Put It On The Windowsill

An Italian-American Family Memoir

Marcia Brennan, Ph.D.

DARK
RIVER

An imprint of Bennion Kearny Ltd.

Published in 2019 by Dark River, an imprint of Bennion Kearny Limited.

Copyright © Dark River

ISBN: 978-1-911121-76-3

Marcia Brennan has asserted her right under the Copyright, Designs and Patents Act, 1988 to be identified as the author of this book.

Published by Dark River, Bennion Kearny Limited
6 Woodside, Churnet View Road
Oakamoor
Staffordshire
ST10 3AE

www.BennionKearny.com

For Nannie and Grandpa,

Maria Concetta and Camillo Gagliardi

Ti Amo
Grazie per il Mondo che Avete Creato per Noi

We Love You
Thank You For the World You Created For Us

ABOUT THE AUTHOR

Marcia Brennan is the Carolyn and Fred McManis Professor of Humanities at Rice University, where she is also Professor of Art History and Religious Studies. She received her B.A. from Mount Holyoke College, and her M.A. and Ph.D. from Brown University. Her research engages the areas of modern and contemporary art history and museum studies, and the medical humanities. She is the author of several books, including *Curating Consciousness: Mysticism and the Modern Museum* (MIT Press, 2010); *Modernism's Masculine Subjects: Matisse, The New York School, and Post-Painterly Abstraction* (MIT Press, 2004); and *Painting Gender, Constructing Theory: The Alfred Stieglitz Circle and American Formalist Aesthetics* (MIT Press, 2001). She is also the co-author of *Modern Mystic: The Art of Hyman Bloom* (New York: Distributed Art Publishers, 2019). She is the winner of the Georgia O'Keeffe Museum Research Center Book Prize, and the recipient of grants from the American Council of Learned Societies, the Office of Research, Rice University, and Rice's Humanities Research Center. She has served as a Fellow at Rice's Center for Teaching Excellence, and in both 2009 and 2010 she was awarded the George R. Brown Award for Superior Teaching. In addition, since early 2009 she has served as an Artist In Residence in the Department of Palliative Care and Rehabilitation Medicine at the M. D. Anderson Cancer Center. Her experiences in this clinical setting represent the subject of her books *The*

Heart of the Hereafter: Love Stories from the End of Life (John Hunt Books, U.K., 2014), *Life at the End of Life: Finding Words Beyond Words* (Intellect Books, U.K. and the University of Chicago Press, 2017), and her current book project *A Rose From Two Gardens: Saint Thérèse of Lisieux and Images of the End of Life* (forthcoming from the University of California Medical Humanities Press).

ACKNOWLEDGEMENTS

First and foremost, this book would not be possible without my father, Alfred Peter Gagliardi. For several years, he has shared stories of the family, many of which are drawn from his own memories. Dad is quoted throughout this book, and the project belongs to him as much as it does to me. Many of the stories also came from my aunt, Theresa Rose Glownia; as you read, she will become an increasingly familiar presence. The other important "ghost author" is my mother, Joan Cosgrove Gagliardi. When my parents first married, my mother wrote Nannie's recipes down by hand. If it were not for her, the recipes would not exist in this form.

From the outset, various family members expressed enthusiasm for the project, and they generously shared their stories. I would like to thank Gene and Kay Bourquin, George and Clare Garner, Nancy and Doug Tracy, Rick and Diana Glownia, Rob Glownia, and Virginia and Fred Larese, as well as my sister Camille Gagliardi and her wife, Dana Gillette. My husband, Scott Brennan, has been wonderful throughout, and he is responsible for all of the contemporary photographs that appear in this book. Good friends and colleagues kindly discussed early versions of the text, and I would like to thank Karen Cottingham, Alex Faris, Donato Loia, Pat McKenna, Marcie Newton, Brian Ogren, Gregory Perron, N. J. Pierce, and Lyn Smallwood. I am grateful to Elias Bongmba, Chair of the Department of Religion at Rice University, for providing support for this project. For his overall guidance and editorial expertise, my gratitude also goes to James Lumsden-Cook, the publisher at Bennion Kearny.

Ultimately, this book is about the world my grandparents created, a world they took with them wherever they went. Thus I would like to thank *all* of my family members (including the ones who are no longer here), and especially, my grandparents Maria Concetta Nesta Gagliardi and Camillo Gagliardi. This book is dedicated to them, in love and gratitude.

TABLE OF CONTENTS

I

THREE WAYS OF APPROACHING A WINDOWSILL: THE MULTIPLE LIVES OF THE STORIES

If You Want Good Weather…

Even though this book is about my extended Italian-American family, I will begin with a story from the Irish side of the family.

I am the oldest of two daughters. On the Irish side, our mother's favorite aunt was our great-aunt, Nanna. Her real name was Anne Cosgrove Boyle, but everyone always called her Nanna. Both Mom and Nanna were devout Catholics, and they were women of extremely strong faith. Once, Aunt Nanna told my mother that, if she wanted good weather for a particular occasion, she should place a statue of the Virgin Mary on the windowsill, facing outward, and say a prayer – and this is just what my mother did.

Statue of the Virgin Mary

The statue of the Virgin Mary was a gift to me from Father Francis, my mother's uncle, who was a parish priest in Connecticut. My mother placed the statue of the Virgin on the pantry windowsill, overlooking the rose arbor in the back yard. In my mind's eye, I can still see this creamy white figure with her back turned toward us, and her serene gaze facing outward, as if she were looking out the window. And yes, when we woke up the next morning, the weather was glorious.

Slam the Window Down, Hard…

The good weather story tells of a prayer and a blessing, and now I'm going to share a story of a curse, which will be followed by a recipe (I promise). Both saints and relatives were very real presences in the house that I grew up in, and they all had distinctive personalities. While Aunt Nanna was sweet and soft-spoken, we had two great-aunts "on the Italian side" who were both vocal and extremely colorful. One was great-aunt Millie, whose real name was Carmella, but who everyone always called Aunt Millie.

While Aunt Millie was a frequent visitor to our house, I only have a vague recollection of the other great-aunt. She was married to my grandmother's younger brother, Uncle Rockie, and everyone always called her Aunt Mary from Hartford. While Aunt Millie could be blunt, Aunt Mary from Hartford could be outrageous. Dad insists that, at heart, Aunt Mary from Hartford was a really good person. Yet she was certainly outspoken, and some of her phrases became legendary in our family. This is one of those phrases, and it is part of a story I was never supposed to have heard, in which Aunt Mary from Hartford offered a hypothetical recipe for solving a practical problem.

One day, the adults were in the living room, talking about one of my father's cousins. This man and his wife had several children within the first few years of their marriage.

3

As one male relative put it, he "kept getting his wife pregnant."[1] When this man announced that he and his wife were expecting another baby, Aunt Mary from Hartford offered a unique response to the news. Did she congratulate him? Oh no. Instead, she told everyone that this man "should put it on the windowsill and slam the window down hard, and that would take care of the problem." She then made a series of accompanying gestures, as if she were acting out this disastrous scenario, slowly lifting up an imaginary window and then bringing it down again, fast and hard – *Bam!*

While all of the adults laughed out loud, I was a bit confused as I tried to get my seven-year-old mind around Aunt Mary from Hartford's idea of "family planning." My thoughts ran something like this: What exactly is she talking about? How would this actually work? And then, a horrified: Oh my God, would anyone ever really *do* such a thing? *She's joking, right?* As I pondered this further, I started to become slightly in awe of the creative inventiveness of her imagery. After all, could a window *really* be used in this way? Who would even *think* of such a thing?

Looking back at this now, I can see that Aunt Mary from Hartford's jarring imagery is nothing short of epiphanic. This is an epiphany because the elements of creation and destruction are interwoven so tightly, and in such a novel fashion, that her curse expresses an inverted sense of humor in response to what should have been a blessing. Her imagery is all about forcefully closing the possibility – or slamming the window down hard – on new life entering the world. Even though I couldn't fully grasp the mechanical

---

[1] Readers today will find some of the phrasings in this book inappropriate, but this is exactly how people expressed themselves in that time and place. In retelling the narratives, I retain the original phrasing in faithfulness to both the wording and the spirit of the stories.

details of this as a child, I did recognize that this was a powerful metaphor, and I knew I was hearing a story that I would never forget. Who the hell could ever forget that one? I'll bet you'll never look at a windowsill the same way again. You can thank Aunt Mary from Hartford for this.

Spinach Pie

Returning to the pantry, when I was a child, people would often put baked goods by windowsills to cool after they came out of the oven. My mother would put breads and cookies on raised silver baking racks on the pantry counter, right by the window where she placed the statue of the Virgin Mary when she wanted good weather. Of all the homemade breads, spinach pie was my favorite. I can still remember the smell of a freshly baked loaf cooling by the pantry windowsill. Like all of the recipes that appear in this book, this recipe can be seen as a fragment of cultural heritage *and* as a formula for creation. (In contrast, the curses are invariably recipes for disaster and destruction!) Mom carefully inscribed the recipe for homemade spinach pie on a 3 x 5 inch index card more than 50 years ago.

Spinach Pie

Ingredients for Filling

Fresh Swiss chard

Olive oil

Chopped green and black olives

Grated parmesan cheese

Garlic salt

Salt

Capers (soak first)

Directions

Mix all ingredients thoroughly in a bowl. Place over bread dough and fold in half, like a turnover. Prick holes with a fork in the top. Bake at 400 degrees until cooked.

Bread Dough

Ingredients

2 ½ lbs. flour

1 tablespoon each salt and sugar (not too full)

¼ yeast cake (approximately)

1 ½ cups water to which add one scant teaspoon of Crisco. Fill to 3 ½ cups, a little better than lukewarm

Directions

Use a Dutch oven. Mix flour, sugar, and salt. Mix well, and add water, dissolving yeast thoroughly. Mix all ingredients, adding water slowly until all ingredients are well mixed. After mixing, knead 10 minutes, turning and tearing mixture as you knead. Wet hands enough to knead. Keep dough warm and well-covered with a dishcloth. After it raises one hour, punch down and let raise another hour. Form into loaves and put in pans (greased with margarine). Let raise another hour until bread reaches top of pan. Then bake for 1 hour at 400 degrees.

Window Magic

The opening stories are all examples of window magic, and they show some of the reciprocal powers of blessings, curses, and creations. The stories allow us to view the ordinary world in symbolic terms. The windowsill provides a little platform to rest on, a convenient perch between various openings and closings, just as the window appears as a transparent membrane conjoining the inner and outer worlds.

Such a conjunction of domains is especially useful if you wish to travel between realms or influence the world in one way or another. In all cases, the windowsill appears as a site for bringing things into being, or for taking things out of being – whether this involves saying a prayer for the creation of a beautiful day, or expressing a desire to close the window on the possibility of bringing more children into the world, or providing a transitional arena before a creation is ready to be consumed.

Why am I telling these stories? For more than a decade, I have served as a literary Artist In Residence in the Department of Palliative Care and Rehabilitation Medicine at the M. D. Anderson Cancer Center in Houston, Texas. My work is sponsored by COLLAGE: The Art for Cancer Network, a nonprofit organization conceived and founded by Dr. Jennifer Wheler. While working in this clinical context, I listen closely as people tell their stories. As we visit together, I record people's words verbatim and then give them back as a gift, inscribing the narratives into handmade paper journals, which the individual and their family are able to keep. When love enters into the stories, the prose often flows like poetry. Then the familiar world appears in a new light, and it begins to take on a life of its own. The heart and knowledge become blended together, and in the subtle intensity of their melding, we are able to glimpse the lives and feel the presences of those who are here, and those who are no longer here. In my own mind, I think of this as the poetry of the in-between. Something similar happens throughout this book.

Thus I wrote this book because I wanted to share my family's story and the magic of this world. While this story will resonate with other Italian-American readers in particular, the book is written for everyone. The tone of voice I adopt is very intimate, as I present a first-person account as I take you inside this world. To paraphrase my father, as you read, you'll just show up, and you'll be welcomed.

In turn, when I do the creative clinical work at M. D. Anderson, I often draw on my childhood experiences as I sit at the bedside and listen as people share the images that are significant to them at the end of their lives.

People will often discuss their homes, their families, their marriages, and their spirituality. They will describe aspects of life that relate to creating a world, and to taking that world with them, wherever they go. Because I have done this clinical work for so many years, I have recorded thousands of stories, and I have written several books on these subjects.[2] Now the time has come to record my family's own stories, particularly as I carry the images so deeply in my mind and heart through multiple aspects of my life. Much like the work I do in the hospital, the stories that appear in this book feature an intriguing mixture of the sacred and the profane. The stories are platforms that create a deeper sense of love and a more cohesive sense of

---

[2] See Marcia Brennan, *The Heart of the Hereafter: Love Stories from the End of Life* (Winchester, UK: John Hunt, 2014); and Marcia Brennan, *Life at the End of Life: Finding Words Beyond Words* (Bristol, UK: Intellect and the University of Chicago Press, 2017). As discussed in the final chapter, a third volume is forthcoming from the University of California Medical Humanities Press.

presence, just as they sit on the windowsill between multiple lives and multiple worlds.

Why Blessings, Curses, and Recipes Are All Spiritual Stories

Whether the stories I tell are religiously-oriented or downright obscene, the blessings and curses are all spiritual stories because they are filled with important insights on human life, just as they demonstrate the art of living in multiple worlds. The approach I adopt in this book is both descriptive and interpretive. Many layers of meaning may be unfolding at once, even if we are not fully aware of everything that is going on at any given moment.

Sometimes, even when nothing appears to be happening, something important may be happening. This too is a significant spiritual *and* life lesson. Each story creates a window into a world that no longer exists, yet which continues on with a life of its own. As we read, we repeatedly pass through these openings, and we encounter the spirit of the stories. Then we experience a sense of what it feels like to be in this world, and to be with someone in spirit.

In recounting the stories, it feels like I have been entrusted with something precious, with a larger sense of cultural memory – a collective presence consisting of a unique time, place, and group of people, some of whom I knew very well and loved dearly, and some of whom I never met. While this book is filled with family histories, the stories also point to something well beyond themselves. All of which is to say that the narratives exist in multiple locations at once.[3] The

---

[3] As a scholar, I have written extensively on the subject of mysticism, which is associated with the capacity to occupy multiple locations simultaneously, to engage transformational elements, and to express transcendent visions. As I tell the stories in this book, a world that no longer exists takes on a life of its own, and thus it exists in another form. I might be tempted to describe this

stories show the gifts of relationships, including those that unfold in the home, in the community, and in cultural heritage. Above all, the stories demonstrate how people can be gifts (and occasionally, curses) to one another. Many of the narratives help us understand perspectives other than our own, just as we recognize that everyone has something of value to offer, and the smallest things in life can sometimes hold the greatest meanings.

Many of the stories engage themes of balance and proportion, and they show how people responded to a sense of lack or excess, scarcity or abundance. Humor is also a key ingredient. Laughter is a type of food, because it feeds the spirit. Much of the humor in this world turned on a sense of unbalancing the status quo, or knowing the world through the flesh. As we all know, some of the best curses come from this sense of embodied knowledge. In turn, many of the blessings involve not only saints and holy figures, but a deeply human sense of altruism that demonstrates how people loved and supported one another. At their very best, the stories show how the magic of the home served as a stage for sacred expressions of love – for *agape,* or a love feast.

Throughout this little book, subheadings appear like logos. Just as logos are commonly used in advertising slogans because the phrases are easy to remember, when capitalized, the term "Logos" expresses a sense of reason through the meaningful use of speech and words.[4] The narratives often

---

transformational element as a type of hermeneutic magic, but I don't want the text to get bogged down in theoretical terms. They don't really belong to this world, and we really don't need them. The transformational magic will speak for itself.

[4] Notably, when capitalized, the term Logos also connotes a sense of divine wisdom that is associated with the creation and the redemption of the world, and which is "often identified with the second person of the Trinity." See the

read like parables, like little stories that provide conceptual frameworks for making sense of otherwise illogical subjects. In short, the blessings repeatedly evoke the presences of saints and holy figures, the curses are funny as hell, and the recipes are delicious. All of which is to say that so many aspects of this world worked like magic. Again and again, the stories show how whole worlds were created out of almost nothing. Not only did our family create these worlds, but they took these worlds with them, wherever they went.

Just as the stories of creations, blessings, and curses appear in a very concentrated form, this little book is like an alembic, like "something that refines or transmutes as if by distillation."[5] As you sit still and read, you get a taste of the spirit of this world. It might evoke something like anisette, the licorice liqueur that my grandmother used to pour in cups of fragrantly brewed coffee when her family came to visit on holiday mornings.

---

entry on "Logos" in *Webster's Seventh New Collegiate Dictionary* (Springfield, MA: G. & C. Merriam, 1969), p. 498.

[5] The definition of "alembic" is found in *Webster's Seventh New Collegiate Dictionary*, p. 21.

Family Trees

My Great-Grandparents and their Children

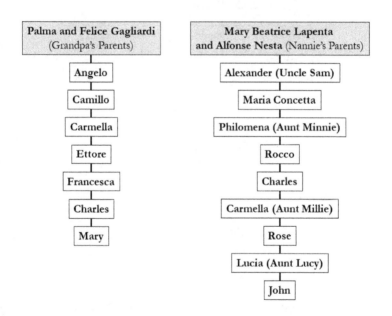

Palma and Felice Gagliardi (Grandpa's Parents)	Mary Beatrice Lapenta and Alfonse Nesta (Nannie's Parents)
Angelo	Alexander (Uncle Sam)
Camillo	Maria Concetta
Carmella	Philomena (Aunt Minnie)
Ettore	Rocco
Francesca	Charles
Charles	Carmella (Aunt Millie)
Mary	Rose
	Lucia (Aunt Lucy)
	John

My Grandparents, their Children and their Spouses, and their
Grandchildren and their Spouses

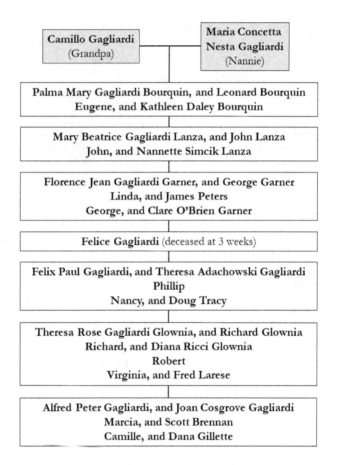

Camillo Gagliardi
(Grandpa)

**Maria Concetta
Nesta Gagliardi**
(Nannie)

**Palma Mary Gagliardi Bourquin, and Leonard Bourquin
Eugene, and Kathleen Daley Bourquin**

**Mary Beatrice Gagliardi Lanza, and John Lanza
John, and Nannette Simcik Lanza**

**Florence Jean Gagliardi Garner, and George Garner
Linda, and James Peters
George, and Clare O'Brien Garner**

Felice Gagliardi (deceased at 3 weeks)

**Felix Paul Gagliardi, and Theresa Adachowski Gagliardi
Phillip
Nancy, and Doug Tracy**

**Theresa Rose Gagliardi Glownia, and Richard Glownia
Richard, and Diana Ricci Glownia
Robert
Virginia, and Fred Larese**

**Alfred Peter Gagliardi, and Joan Cosgrove Gagliardi
Marcia, and Scott Brennan
Camille, and Dana Gillette**

II

BOTH ITALIAN AND AMERICAN: MULTIPLE LIVES IN MULTIPLE WORLDS

See – She Knows!

My grandmother's full name was Maria Concetta Nesta Gagliardi, but everyone always called her Nannie. Nannie's mother was three years old when her family came to the United States from the Avellino Provence, near Naples. Her full name was Mary Beatrice (in English), and Maria Battista (in Italian). While she passed away when Dad was only seven, he recalls that my great-grandmother ran a grocery store on the family property, and that she would sometimes feed children there. He also remembers that, "When people were having babies, she would assist. She was not trained as a midwife, but when people were having babies they would say, 'Go get Zia [Aunt] Battiste.' I think they'd call on her for a lot of things."

Nannie was born on March 22, 1901, the oldest daughter of nine children. Nannie was the matriarch of our extended family, and my father was the youngest of her six living children. I grew up in the three-family house that my grandfather built in New Britain, Connecticut, in 1926. My parents lived on the ground floor, Nannie lived on the second floor, and the third floor was rented out to tenants.

The home was like an intricate living work of art that our grandparents created together. However, this chapter is not yet about my grandparents' shared world. Instead, this chapter tells the stories of before the beginning, and after the end, of Nannie and Grandpa's 42-year marriage.

While I was growing up, Nannie's home was a magnet, and not just for our family. *Everyone* would come to visit Nannie. Even when distant acquaintances from Europe came to visit their relatives in the United States, at some point in their travels they would stop by to see Nannie. As a child, I could slip seamlessly between the first and second floors of the house, between my parents' world and my grandparents'. Upstairs, the adults would be sitting in the living room talking, and I could glide in through the kitchen screen door, pass through the thickly carpeted dining room, and land on the little golden footstool by Nannie's wing chair. I did this so often and so fluidly that sometimes it would be several minutes before I was even noticed. This was especially the case when the adults were deep in conversation.

In appearance, I was tall and thin, with pale skin and long auburn hair. All of which is to say that I didn't exactly look Italian. Nannie's visitors would speak in a mixture of Italian and English, and I could generally follow the conversations without too much trouble. The bottom line is that I knew far more than they thought I did.

As their discussions progressed, I often remained invisible until I either smiled or laughed at some key point in the story. And then, the older person would glance over at me and recognize – by the look on my face – that I had understood exactly what was being said, and that I was *really interested* in knowing what happened between the woman from church, and the man who lived next door… Then the visitor would smile knowingly at Nannie. They would nod and cock their head in my direction and say, "See – she knows!"

What Could My Answer Be, But Yes?

My parents first met in September of 1963, through their work in the Connecticut public school system. Before the school term started, all of the teachers were required to attend a morning meeting. Approximately 500 people were present, and the new teachers were told to stay for a luncheon. Dad did not know anyone there, but he said to himself, "I'm going to find a girl to eat with." He did more than this; he found the girl he would marry. My parents soon discovered that they were assigned to the same middle school, where Dad was an Industrial Arts teacher, and Mom was the school librarian. They became friends and, after a little while, Dad wrote a note asking Mom for a date. He left the note in her mailbox at school. The next morning she came down to his classroom and said, "What could my answer be but, yes?" They were married two years later, on August 21, 1965.

Like so many families living in the Northeast and mid-Atlantic regions during the twentieth century, my family was of mixed European heritage. And, the two sides of the family came from really different worlds. While my father's family was of Italian heritage, my mother came from an Irish-American family. This family was very formal and well-to-do. Each Sunday was spent at my maternal grandparents' home in North Haven, Connecticut. These afternoons evoke memories of mink coats and white gloves and cocktails, of quiet rooms where heavy drapes kept out the afternoon sunlight, while a crossword puzzle book sat open on the living room hassock. Dinners and special events were held at not one but two of Connecticut's oldest and most prestigious country clubs, the New Haven Country Club and the Race Brook Country Club, where my mother's family were lifetime members. This was the Irish side of the family, and this book is not really about them. That's another family, that's another book, and yes, that's another story.

My Mother's Wedding Portrait

My Parents' Wedding Party, August 21, 1965

As this brief description suggests, my sister Camille and I grew up with the sense of double vision that comes from living in two families, two cultures, and two worlds. Just as we lived in these multiple worlds, we also spent a great deal of time traveling between them, passing from one realm to another. These transitions were certainly not easy. Despite their differences, both sides of the family held extremely conservative social, cultural, and religious worldviews, and it is a masterpiece of an understatement to say that, for many years, we all challenged one another. Yet, while growing up in these worlds, I learned many valuable lessons that have lasted a lifetime, and for which I am extremely grateful.

My Mother holding Camille and myself

Holding Onto the Best

My family history can thus be situated within a much broader, rapidly shifting, social context. Many of these larger patterns concerned the tightening and loosening of the boundaries between various domains. During the early- and mid-twentieth century, so much of my grandparents' world depended on the traditional values associated with solidified conceptions of identity and community. The virtues of this world centered on a consolidated sense of strength and purpose, which became reaffirmed and reinforced as people created a life together and supported one another within it. Yet, as I became a teenager and a young adult during the 1980s and 1990s, American culture moved from the modern to the postmodern era. Instead of the firm boundaries that delineated a traditional world, my era was very much about the conscious erosion of those same boundaries.

During these transitional decades, everything was becoming fluid and porous, hybrid and composite – and these broader changes unfolded on numerous levels at once, socially and culturally, personally and politically. These were necessary and valuable developments, although such rapid changes inevitably carried their own losses. On the positive side, these larger trends created a greater sense of equity and inclusion, openness and expansiveness, and with them, opportunities for freedom and growth associated with an enlarged vision of the world. Yet these shifts also brought the loss of a stable sense of community, as well as the positive *and* negative values on which such communities were built. Conjoining both lights and shadows, one of the realities of this world was that individuals whose lives – for whatever reason – fell outside of the boundaries of the traditional cultural narratives could not be fully integrated within them. Our own family's hybrid story exemplifies so many of these complicated themes. Thus one of the most pressing questions that remain for me is: how is it possible to acknowledge these issues and still hold onto the best of everything? As I tell the stories, I begin to bridge multiple worlds, at least on the symbolic level. And if I am very lucky, I manage to re-create something of the world my grandparents created.

Both sides of the family shared a devout sense of Roman Catholicism. Growing up during the 1970s, Camille and I went through eight years of Catholic school. Saint Joseph's School was the elementary and middle school associated with the local parish church. Our father is a lifelong parishioner there, and for many decades, he served as a member of Parish Council and a Minister of the Eucharist. When I was a little girl, Nannie told me that she also went to Saint Joseph's School, which she attended through the eighth grade. Nannie particularly recalled that "the nuns were so strict." Saint Joseph's Church was founded in 1896, and the school was initially located in its attic. The house that Nannie grew up in was originally the church's rectory. Nannie's father bought the house from the church, and after my great-grandfather and his friends hand-dug the foundation, the building was moved to its new location by horses. This is where my grandmother lived until she married my grandfather on February 19, 1919, a month before her eighteenth birthday.

Pa Would Have Loved You Kids

Our paternal grandfather's name was Camillo Gagliardi. His friends called him Cammie, Nannie and Dad called him Pa, and Camille and I always referred to him as Grandpa. Grandpa was born in 1895 in the village of Pedivigliano, within the province of Cosenza, in the region of Calabria. He came to the United States in 1913, when he was 17 years old. Grandpa crossed with his cousin, our great-uncle Henry Funari.

Uncle Henry later married Nannie's sister, Aunt Minnie (whose real name was Philomena). Dad told me that, "In order to sail, Uncle Henry had to get his father's permission. Uncle Henry and his father were like oil and water, so Pa told him not to antagonize his father, and he went over with him when it was time to sign the piece of paper" that allowed Uncle Henry and Grandpa to travel to America. Even as a teenager, my grandfather helped to arrange things diplomatically. The two young men sailed on the ship *Ancona*, which passed through New York's storied Ellis Island.[6] Grandpa's oldest brother, Angelo, had come to this country first, and Grandpa lived with him when he first arrived. Grandpa was one of seven children, all but one of whom settled in America. Another brother, Ettore, remained in Italy, and he came to this country to visit.

While Nannie was a constant presence during my childhood, our grandfather passed away two years before my parents ever met. Thus, my knowledge of Grandpa comes through the stories, photographs, and stray traces of his presence that remained like relics in Nannie's home. These included the handful of toiletry items that always stood tenderly in Nannie's bathroom, on the shelf just to the right of the mirror. Growing up, Grandpa was thus a subtle absent presence, and I always wondered about him – who was he, what was he like, and most importantly, would he have liked my sister and myself? Whenever I asked about him, Nannie would always begin by reassuring me, "Pa would have loved you kids!"

---

[6] According to the official passenger record, our grandfather's "last place of residence" is listed as Pedegliano. Our grandfather's passenger record can be found on the webpage of The Statue of Liberty—Ellis Island Foundation, Inc. at:
https://www.libertyellisfoundation.org/passenger-result

Grandpa was a beloved presence in our family. While I never had the opportunity to meet him, our cousin Rick generously shared his recollection of our grandfather:

Grandpa was an amazing man.
He died on my 7th birthday,
But I have very fond memories of him.
The most vivid memory was just before he died.
He was at home on Kensington Avenue.

Everyone had gone to see him,
And I had to sit out on the stairs
Going up to the second floor.
I wasn't allowed in to see him.
I started crying.
To this day, I remember saying,
"He's my Grandpa.
I need to see him."

Nannie heard me,
And she took me into the bedroom
For a very quick minute.
That was the last I saw him.
He died a couple of days later.

Now it's 58 years later,
And it seems like it just happened.

Rick also recalls how, when he and his brother Rob were very small, they would play carpenters in the back yard. As pretend carpenters, Rob was called Joe, and Rick went by the name of Pete. One day, Grandpa walked up to the house for a visit. As he came up the driveway, he heard the two little boys playing, and he stood to watch them for a moment. Apparently, Grandpa got a kick out of Rick calling his brother Joe, so Grandpa also started calling Rob, Joe. Rick remembers that, when Rob was only three or four years old, he must have done something to mildly upset Grandpa. Speaking in a thick Italian accent in broken English, Grandpa said to little Rob, "I love you Joe, but geez you tick." In this world, "tick" (or thick) meant stubborn. Both the phrase and the nickname stuck for many years. To this day, Rick still sometimes calls his brother Joe. When the right moment arises, I will have to remind Rob, "geez, you tick."

That's How That Worked

A few years ago, I asked Dad to tell me about his father – what he was like, and what he remembered the most. As Dad spoke, another fragment of family history emerged. Dad's full name is Alfred Peter Gagliardi, and his birthday is June 29th. These details are significant because Catholic saints enter into this story, along with the existential details of people who lived their lives in multiple worlds. Much like our grandfather, this story is also multiple – it is both Italian and American. Dad's narrative is like a window into life on two continents:

Pa considered himself both Italian and American.
He had American citizenship.
He went back to Italy in 1948,
And he stayed for three months.
While Pa was in Italy, every Saturday night,
My godfather, Goomba Pippie, came to stay with Nannie
At the store, back in the United States, until closing time.
He didn't want her there alone,
And he did this for three months.
Those people looked after each other.

I was only twelve then.
Pa took the boat *Saturnia* –
It was a big deal to make that trip.
They shipped steamer trunks.
They left either at the end of May
Or the beginning of June,
And they stayed about three months.

Sam Costanza and he were from the same village,
And they traveled together.
Over here, Sam and he took up a collection
And they brought the money with them.
In their village, the church had a bell that was cracked.
They had the bell redone,
And they had a feast for the town
On Saint Peter's Day, which is my birthday.
They replaced the bell, and they had this feast.
Saint Peter was the patron saint of the town.
They engraved the names of everybody
Who donated on the bell.
The village is Pedivigliano, in the Cosenza Province,
In Calabria.
Sam Costanza took a picture of the cracked bell.
I don't know what happened to it – Auntie Florie had it.

My father liked to play bocce,
And he played while he was there.
They named the bocce court after him, after he left.
Some years later, they also raised money
For something the church didn't have –
A baptismal font.
I gave money for that,
In honor of my father.

Those people stuck together
And they helped each other out.
That's how that worked.

While Dad's account was matter-of-fact, his voice was filled with pride and tenderness as he spoke of his father and of their shared culture. Just as this sense of multiplicity means different things for members of different generations, the multiple perspectives embedded in this story create space for more life, both Italian and American.

Thank God We Made It Without Being Blown Up

The story of our grandfather's journey to and from Italy does not end there – and the next part of the narrative is far less poetic. Dad told me that, when Grandpa returned from Italy, he brought home a steamer trunk filled with gifts for everyone (including various items of contraband Italian food, which I'm still not supposed to mention, even though this occurred over 70 years ago). The journey home was almost as much of an adventure as the trip itself. When our grandfather's ship *Saturnia* entered the Port of New York, it took many hours before the family ever saw Grandpa.[7] During the passage, someone had died, and all of the passengers had to be inoculated before they were allowed to disembark. Then, the porters had misfiled Grandpa's steamer trunk, placing it under the letter "C" (for his first name, Camillo) instead of "G" (for Gagliardi), and this also took time to sort out. Yet the journey was not over—there was still the car trip back to Connecticut. Although Dad was only twelve, he vividly recalled:

> When it was time for your grandfather and
> Sam Costanza to come home from Italy,
> Sam's father went to see Nannie, and he said,

---

[7] At the time of our grandfather's sailing, the *Saturnia* had just entered into commercial service for post-war voyages. Regarding the history of the ship, see: https://www.italianliners.com/saturnia-en

"I'm taking you and your son to New York
To pick up your husband and my son."

While we were going to New York from Connecticut,
The car stalled on the Merritt Parkway,
And it had to be pushed to be restarted.
It's a good thing we didn't get killed.
We didn't know it at the time,
But raw gasoline was dripping on the hot engine.

In New York, Nannie went to meet
The passengers at the dock,
And Sam's father brought the car into a shop to be fixed.
The guys at the shop must have seen
The Connecticut license plates,
And thought they had an easy mark,
Because they wanted to charge over $38
To do the repair job.
This would be like a week's wages at the time.
So Mr. Costanza said no,
And he brought the car back home.

It turned out that, rather than needing an entire engine replacement as the garage had said, the needle had gotten stuck by the carburetor, and it just had to be tapped back into place. As Dad said, "Can you imagine, they wanted to charge him all that money?" Hearing this, I replied, "Yes, but… it really wasn't safe to drive the car all that way in that condition. I mean, what if something serious had happened?" I started to get concerned about this situation, yet Dad was totally cool about the whole thing. Hearing the anxiety creep into my voice, he calmly replied, "Yeah. Thank God we made it without being blown up."

My Great-Grandfather Could Write

On two different occasions, spaced several decades apart, both Dad's sister, Auntie Theresa, and our second cousin, Mary Falvo, told me that Grandpa's father – our great-grandfather in Italy – could write, and that he used to write poetry. Auntie Theresa then told me that, as a child, she also wrote poems. When she was in the first grade, one of the first poems she ever wrote was typed up on a sheet of composition paper and placed on the bulletin board in the main hallway of her elementary school. She remembered this clearly because the experience made such an impression on her. As she said, "They didn't just do this for everyone." The incident was important because, in childhood, it showed her one of her gifts, and the type of creativity she was capable of. During this conversation, Auntie Theresa also told me that, when our grandfather emigrated to this country, he brought some of his father's poems with him, but they were in a steamer trunk that was lost. Dad later confirmed this story. He said, "Your great-grandfather could write. I think he was a poet. But, he didn't make a living at that. He was a shoemaker, and so was my uncle Ettore, the brother who stayed in Italy." Thus according to three different family members, our great-grandfather was a shoemaker who wrote poetry. I can imagine him sitting in his shop, stitching words together as he made the shoes that people wore as they walked into and out of his world.

I Can Feel a Part of Them, Too

When Grandpa died, our father went into a deep state of mourning. Even though Nannie had just lost her husband, this did not prevent her from being a good mother to her son. She shared wisdom regarding not only Grandpa, but all of the relatives who had passed on. As Nannie told Dad, "Just remember, all of those people had to lose their parents, too."

This was brilliant, and not only because Nannie's kind words comforted Dad. Through this statement, Nannie turned a curse into a blessing. Even though our father had just experienced a heartbreaking loss, Nannie still found a way to open his eyes and his heart, so that he could feel closer to his father. Moreover, while facing loss and grief, Nannie taught Dad how to have compassion for humanity itself. Her words came as a gift, when such a gift was most needed. By adopting this larger perspective, Dad could see that people who were no longer here were human beings who experienced both suffering and joy, and he could recognize that we all had something so deep and tender in common. Dad never forgot Nannie's words, and I have not forgotten them, either. They changed the way my father – and I – look at death, and at life itself.

Dad's conversation with Nannie occurred nearly six decades ago. Dad has told me that he now realizes he is the last living male relative of his generation, as the rest have passed on. I replied that, while hearing the family stories, I feel like a part of them are here with us now. Dad immediately responded, "I can feel a part of them, too." While so many of these events happened so many decades ago, when we read the stories, we get a subtle sense of the world our family created. And, like Dad, we can feel a part of them, too.

III

YOU COULD EAT OFF THE FLOOR: HOW MY GRANDPARENTS CREATED A WORLD, AND HOW THEY TOOK THAT WORLD WITH THEM, WHEREVER THEY WENT

Unless you somehow had inside access to this culture, you could never fully know what it meant to live in a twentieth-century, Italian-American home. Many of the people who lived in this world began with almost nothing, and they skillfully created lives they deeply cherished. Homemaking was both an art and a craft, and it was the work of a lifetime. Such worlds no longer exist in quite these forms today. You really had to have been there to witness the vast amounts of time and effort, artistry and care, that went into the creation and maintenance of these remarkable worlds.

No Sporcaccione!

First and foremost, everything was incredibly clean. And I don't just mean clean – I mean *sparkling and immaculate.* Imagine the most spotless environment you've ever been in, and then triple it. Envision scenes of gleaming white enamel cooking surfaces, highly polished woodwork, flawless expanses of smooth neutral carpeting, crisply starched yet still incredibly soft linens, and endless rows of colorful flowered dishes all neatly stacked on pantry shelves, where light beams in through transparent glass windowpanes. These spaces were magical, and growing up in such a world was a blessing. Yet this blessing also carried an accompanying curse, much like a twin who remained a silent partner until she started speaking, and always in Italian.

Let's begin with some humor. The joke about these houses was that everything was so clean, you could eat off the floor. Not that anyone ever did this, of course. But honestly, you could have. Cooking and food were as sacred as the house itself, and one of the greatest compliments you could ever pay someone was to bring your two hands outward in a wide, sweeping gesture that encompassed the totality of the universe, and emphatically proclaim: **You could eat off their floor!** This phrase was a blessing, and it was always expressed in English.

In contrast, one of the worst curses you could ever throw at someone (or at their entire family) was to say that they were *sporcaccione*. *Sporcaccione* is an extremely interesting word, in part because it knows no boundaries. The term implies someone or something that is not just dirty, but absolutely filthy and completely disgusting.[8] In conversational usage, *sporcaccione* is an adjective that means to be like a pig – and thus, to be like an animal that poops and eats in the same location in its own little pigpen. Even worse, the animal doesn't have the sense to know any better. Thus *sporcaccione* simultaneously connotes a lapse in judgment as well as in hygiene, and it indicates a person who will never fully be trusted. Yet the most interesting aspect of this concept is that, somehow, these extremes were always crystal clear to everyone, and there was no room for ambiguity or argument. In this world, either you were filthy, or you were immaculate. Either you were *sporcaccione*, or you could eat off the floor. There was no wiggle room for oinking out any sort of appeal or negotiation.

What this meant in practical terms was that, if you were a member of the younger generation, and an extremely busy professional woman, you still did not get a pass. Oh no, the relatives had something else lined up for you. While you were not overtly criticized, during a visit they would simply come into your kitchen *and start cleaning things of their own accord.* And by this, I don't mean that they would just help out in a nice friendly way and casually wash some dishes. Oh no – nothing ever began or ended there. Instead, they would put on yellow rubber gloves, whip out a can of oven cleaner, and start scrubbing away like there was no tomorrow. They would do this like it was the most natural

---

[8] For the definitions of the Italian words appearing in this book, I have consulted Robert C. Melzi, *The Bantam New College Italian & English Dictionary* (New York: Bantam Books, 1976).

thing in the world. And for them, it probably was. *No more sporcaccione!* By the time the visit was over, you were completely exhausted, but everything was so clean you could eat off the floor. All that cleaning was something like the cleansing of a curse. It was a kind of atonement, like washing away the sins of the spaghetti sauce. Rather than going to church and confessing to the priest, this was a do-it-yourself form of absolution for the sins of domestic omission: Say two Hail Marys, and buy another can of oven cleaner.

Looking back at all of this, a part of me is still wondering: *Just what the hell was going on in the kitchen?* Yet I've also learned to view these things symbolically, and to maintain a sense of humor. Laughter is knowledge, and it's a powerful tool when maintaining multiple perspectives. If we were to look at this situation metaphorically, the image of "eating off the floor" is an inversion that turns the lowest into the highest, so that a curse becomes a blessing that affirms the sacredness of the home. This insight goes a long way toward explaining why so much time and effort were devoted to doing all that housework. The bottom line is that the home and the family were the material expressions of the life people created together, and this world meant everything, from the very beginning.

Hello Gal!

Dad told me that, during the 1910s, almost no one had cars. The joke was that, in those days, the only people who had cars were the local doctors and the Italian young men who formed my grandfather's circle of friends and family. These young men pooled their resources together, and they shared a car. In those days, in order to get a driver's license you had to go to Hartford and tell the clerk how much you had driven. If you had driven a certain number of hours, then you got a license. Grandpa got his driver's license very soon after coming to this country, but Nannie never learned to drive. Dad told me that, not a lot of women of that generation ever did learn. In contrast, the men *loved* their cars. Most of them were European craftsmen and tradesmen who worked with their hands, whether it was in tailoring, shoemaking, construction, or mechanical work. While Dad does not know the type of car that his father and their friends first drove, he clearly remembers that, later on, one of the uncles turned a Model A Ford into a racing car. When it came time to register the car, they found they couldn't. Because it was a sports car, the car did not have a windshield, and this was a necessary element for automotive registration. Dad recalls that this particular car was red, and that the men fixed it up so that it resembled a boat that tapered at both the front and back ends. Yet well before this custom-made, unregistered boat of a red sports car ever came into existence, there was the car that Grandpa and his friends shared. Nannie told Dad that this group of young men liked to drive around town, ride by the girls, and call out, "Hello Gal!"

Will You Be My Maid of Honor?

Thankfully, this is not the story of how my grandparents first met. Their first meeting was a blessing in which one wedding inspired another. As a teenager, Nannie worked for a short time at a local factory, the P&F Corbin Company, which manufactured decorative hardware. Nannie's father did factory work, but because Nannie was the oldest girl, and there were several young children in the family, her father told her, "Your job is at home." While Nannie only worked at the factory a few short weeks, in that brief time she met a young woman named Ernestine, and they became good friends. In fact, they became such good friends that Ernestine asked Nannie, "Will you be my maid of honor when I get married?", and Nannie said yes. A little while later, Ernestine married Grandpa's older brother, Angelo.

At the wedding, Nannie was Aunt Ernestine's maid of honor, and Grandpa was Uncle Angelo's best man.

Dad told me that his parents "were a good match because they created such a good balance together." Nannie was conservative, and Grandpa was a risk-taker. Yet when it came time to ask Nannie to marry him, Grandpa took no risks at all. Once again, when approaching such important life decisions, my grandfather acted diplomatically. He enlisted the aid of a go-between, a man named Frank Bosco. Mr. Bosco was a *Paesano*, a fellow country-man who was well-respected. This man was a barber who, according to Dad, "had influence in the neighborhood. So, your grandpa asked Bosco to speak to Nannie's father about the marriage."

We are extremely fortunate to have a photograph showing two young couples standing together, arm in arm, by the side of a wooden house. On the right are Uncle Angelo and his wife, Aunt Ernestine, while Grandpa and Nannie are on the left. Both couples are formally dressed. The women wear long skirts with white lace blouses, and little floral corsages tucked just above their interlinked arms. The men wear three-piece suits over white shirts with high collars, knotted neckties, and gold watch chains. They have little smiles on their faces, and so they should. This photograph was taken the day my grandparents became engaged. Looking into the face of a grandfather I never met, I see my father's features so clearly. Looking at Nannie, I see the very young face of a woman I knew so well and loved so deeply. This photograph marks the beginning of my grandparents' life together.

Grandpa and Nannie, Aunt Ernestine and Uncle Angelo, taken on the day that Nannie and Grandpa became engaged

Everything Was Like a Miniature Work of Art

Just as the story of my grandparents' engagement reflects the protocols associated with traditional gestures of respect, their union was situated securely within their community and their culture. Once again, this world was multiple. It was both Italian and American, and this sense of multiplicity lay at the foundation of the world they created together. In this world, weddings are literally sacred events. They are celebrations of the Sacrament of Matrimony, a ritual that begins in the church and ends in the home. Food is central to the occasion, and weddings bring out some of the most elaborate foods of all. In my grandparents' day, the weddings were held at the local parish church, Saint Joseph's Church, and the receptions were held at the bride's family's house. Both friends and relatives cooked for the occasion.

As is still the case today, the wedding cake is central at these events. Dad told me that, "In the old days, the wedding cake was always a fruit cake. That was tradition." He described how the cake would be made in tiers and frosted with white icing. Inside, the cake was brown, and it was filled with candied fruit. As Dad observed, "In the old days, you couldn't just go to a grocery store and buy chopped candied fruit, like you can today. You would have to go to the Italian store." Dad recalled that there were at least two such stores in downtown New Britain, where "the fruit would come in huge pieces, and you would have to cut it up to make the cake." One of Nannie's younger sisters, great-aunt Lucy, made such wedding cakes, including the cake for my parents' wedding. Traditional weddings also featured elaborate trays of Italian cookies interspersed with colorful Jordan almonds. Some of the cookies were filled, some were plain, and all were extremely beautiful.

Italian cookies are not just for weddings, and they can turn any occasion into something very special. I remember the summer day my family took a trip to Gillette Castle State Park. We packed a picnic lunch and, on the way, Nannie instructed Dad to stop at the bakery and buy a box of Italian cookies. Nannie's treat transformed the picnic into a feast. During a recent visit to my parents' home, Dad bought a similar box of Italian cookies from a traditional bakery in town. After dinner, the cookies were placed in the dining room on a piece of my parents' flowered wedding china. The china was a gift from Dad's four sisters, nearly 50 years before. Like so many things in that world, even the smallest details of life appeared like miniature works of art.

Traditional Italian cookies served on my
parents' wedding china

Italian White Cookies

Ingredients

12 eggs

2 cups sugar

1 pound Crisco, slightly softened (2 cups)

4 tablespoons baking powder

2 teaspoons vanilla or other flavoring

12 cups flour (3 pounds)

Directions

Beat eggs until frothy. The more you beat the eggs, the better. Add sugar, cooled Crisco, baking powder, and flavoring.

Add flour a little at a time. After you have added all the flour, you will have to use your hands to mix the dough. Roll out on a floured board and form into different shapes. Place on greased pans.

Bake at 350 degrees for 15-20 minutes. Undercook. Never over-cook the cookies.

Shoveling a Path to the Wedding

Nannie and Grandpa were married on February 19, 1919. Shortly before the wedding, a multi-day blizzard struck. The city did not have snow plows or other mechanized vehicles to clear the roads or sidewalks, so Grandpa and his friends took matters into their own hands. They manually shoveled a path from Nannie's house to Saint Joseph's Church. According to Dad, "It took Pa and his friends a couple of days to do this, and they made a path of 300 to 400 feet. All the men shoveled so that your grandmother could get to church." From the very beginning, the members of the community supported one another. They literally battled the elements to clear a pathway to the wedding, and to the beginning of my grandparents' married life together.

Good Friends Are Better Than Money

By trade, my grandfather was a tailor, as was his youngest brother, Uncle Charlie. In their hometown in Calabria, boys learned the trade by being apprenticed in the shop of a master craftsman. In America, Grandpa's tailor shop was situated in a corner storefront on the street level of an apartment building that he and Nannie owned. This building was always referred to as "the block." Around the corner was the shop of another tailor, Francisco Choto. Mr. Choto and my grandfather apprenticed together in Italy, and they were friends in the United States. In addition to making custom suits and doing repairs and alterations, Grandpa and his business partner, Jack Badal, would drive into New York City, to a place called Burnham's, where they would buy men's clothes to sell in their own tailor shop. The shop was one of three businesses on the ground floor of the building. There was also a shoemaker's shop and, after Prohibition ended in 1933, a liquor store.

When the building was eight years old, Grandpa and Uncle Angelo bought the block together as partners. Nannie and Grandpa later bought out Uncle Angelo and Aunt Ernestine's share of the property. Like his father, Uncle Angelo was a shoemaker, but his store was not located in the block. This building was also the place where the families lived when Nannie and Grandpa were first married. Six apartments were located above the stores. In addition to Nannie and Grandpa, Uncle Angelo and Aunt Ernestine lived in another apartment, as did Grandpa's business partner Jack and his wife Jane. At different times, various relatives lived in other units. Many years after Grandpa retired, his partner was still working as a tailor. Dad brought him a raincoat for alterations, but Jack wouldn't accept any money for the job. As he told Dad, "Good friends are better than money."

Like Shiny New Pins

Nannie and Grandpa lived in the block until 1926, when they built a three-family house in a residential section of town. And it was there, for the rest of their married life together, that my grandparents created a world. While there was a certain amount of overlap between their domains, Nannie's world was primarily situated inside of the house, while Grandpa's world was located outside of it.

When I was a little girl, I once told Nannie how clean and shiny her home always looked. Nannie smiled, and she told me a story. Many decades before, a lady from her children's school had come to visit. My aunts were only young girls at the time, and they were all dressed up and they looked very nice. The woman glanced over admiringly at the girls and said to Nannie, "Your children look just like shiny new pins in a brand new pin box." Even though this had occurred several decades before, Nannie always remembered the woman's comment, and she still glowed with pride, for herself and her family.

Yet the bright lights and blessings of this world also had their corresponding shadows. Indeed, there were special Italian names for people who were sloppy or ill-kempt. These imaginary figures were called *Maria Sciabagone* and *Maria Scialarelle*. The two Marias didn't actually exist, although I think the first Maria's name is an adaptation of *sciatta*, which means sloppy or slovenly, while the second Maria may be a variation of *scialare*, which denotes someone who is spendthrift or wasteful with money. These two allegorical figures always traveled together, and as children, we always knew what the names implied. My cousin Ginnie has a great sense of humor, much like her mother, Auntie Theresa. A few years ago, I asked Ginnie if she had any idea where these imaginary figures came from, or who *Maria Scialarelle* even was? Without missing a beat, Ginnie looked at me with a very serious expression and said, "Well Marcia, I guess *Maria Scialarelle* hangs out with *Maria Sciabagone*." And then we both started laughing. After all, none of this really made sense and we knew it. We were living in a world with a logic all its own.

Go Out to the Garden and Get a Handful of Parsley

Nannie had a green thumb, and her living room opened directly onto a sun parlor: an airy room with windows running along its three sides. The sun parlor held several pieces of white wicker furniture, including a large plant stand filled with lush green plants. The sun parlor was the place where Nannie rested, and I loved spending time reading quietly in this room. Yet most of the time, the real action would be in the kitchen. Nannie was a creative artist with food. While I am not a cook, as a child I spent countless hours sitting at Nannie's kitchen table, watching closely as she made all types of homemade dishes. I also helped out with small jobs. One of my regular tasks was to go out to the back garden and gather fresh herbs and vegetables, and then bring them into the kitchen so that

Nannie could cook with them. Depending on what was in season and what Nannie happened to be making that day, the fresh vegetables could be tomatoes, lettuce, peppers, green beans, or Swiss chard, while the herbs could be basil, oregano, parsley, or spearmint if it was summertime and we were having iced tea. The house also had a wine cellar in the basement, a cool darkened spot where bottles of wine, baskets of apples, and sacks of potatoes were stored. I would sometimes be sent down there to bring things up to the kitchen. There was a gas stove in the basement, and Nannie would use this area as a second kitchen. The stove was especially handy for fried foods – such as fried dough, or the angel wings and honey cookies she would make at Christmastime – as well as for canning the garden tomatoes that would be put in clear glass jars and later used to make fresh tomato sauce. Dad recalls that Nannie and Grandpa also used the stove in the cellar to make homemade sausage with fennel.

Pickled Tomatoes or Peppers

Use 2 parts water to 1 part white vinegar. Wash tomatoes and bottles. Put tomatoes in bottles, and add 1 teaspoon of salt to the quart, 1/8 teaspoon of alum, ½ clove of garlic, ½ teaspoon fennel seed. Pour boiling vinegar-water mixture over it, and cover tightly.

Invert bottles in a shallow pan with water. Let boil a few minutes.

For peppers, add 1 teaspoon sugar.

You Can Always Put Something In, But Once It's In, You Can Never Take It Out Again

Nannie never used a recipe. She worked exclusively by eye and by touch, and her cooking was informed by a lifetime's worth of skill and knowledge. She knew how to expertly mix and blend ingredients together in just the right amounts, and she applied this same method when creating a world. Just as Nannie's world exemplified a balanced and grounded approach to life, cooking was the material expression of an entire philosophy of living. As she prepared the dough for homemade pasta, Nannie repeated various lessons as she worked. While carefully mixing a pinch of salt into the sifted flour, Nannie would hold the ingredients out in her hand and say, "You can always add more. You can always put something in, but once it's in, you can never take it out again." The lesson would then be repeated as Nannie mixed chopped parsley into freshly beaten egg yolks, creating a wet mixture that would be combined with the dry ingredients. Nannie expressed similar lessons while she blended the breadcrumbs, hand-grated parmesan cheese, egg yolks, parsley, salt, and pepper to create the mixture that would be added to the hamburger for *polpetts,* the flat homemade Italian meatballs that she would pan-fry and add to tomato sauce.

Meatballs

Ingredients

Hamburger

Garlic (small clove, or garlic salt)

Parsley

Bread (soaked and squeezed)

Grated cheese (approximately 1 ½ handfuls)

Crumbled basil leaves

Oregano

Salt

Pepper

2 eggs per pound of hamburger

Directions

Make flat meatballs from the above and fry out in some olive oil. Fry onion (diced) in same oil. Add ½ can tomato paste. Make smooth. Put in saucepan. Add 1 can of water in fry pan, and add to saucepan. Add tomatoes and parsley. Add ½ teaspoon sugar.

Cook ½ hour. Add meatballs. Cook 1 hour longer, then turn off. Add water if sauce gets thick.

Nannie mixed many of these same ingredients together to create the batter she used to coat yellow squash flowers, which would be picked fresh from the garden, dipped into the mixture, and lightly pan-fried on the stovetop until they were golden brown. Dad told me that the idea for this recipe came from Mary and Paul Falvo, who grew beautiful squash in their garden. Just as Nannie was always cooking, she was always carefully observing and blending, while teaching the fine points of balance and proportion. And, as she worked, she held everything so tenderly in her hands.

Giambotta: If You Could Eat It, It Was a Blessing; If You Had to Clean It Up, It Was a Curse

Just as everything in Nannie's home was in beautiful order, my family had another colorful expression for something that was disorderly. If a situation was a total mess, it was like *giambotta* – and yes, this is another example in which food takes on a metaphorical life of its own. *Giambotta* is literally a traditional vegetable dish that I think of as a cultural heritage food. As Dad observed, *giambotta* was made from "whatever we would have in the garden." It is a kind of in-between dish. It is not exactly a soup, but it's also not exactly a vegetable medley. It's a kind of colorful, fresh vegetable stew that Nannie served in a soup bowl, and it was composed of tomatoes, squash, beans, and zucchini, as well as fresh parsley and oregano.

Giambotta is literally a mish-mash. The Italian word relates to *gimboi-co*, which means a jumble. *Giambotta* thus serves as a versatile metaphor for a state of total confusion. Moreover, *giambotta* not only means the mess itself, but it could signify the process of someone making a mess and mixing things up, especially if they did so in a careless way – or, God forbid – if they acted in total negligence. Conversationally, the term could be used as a kind of prohibition or warning, as in: "No make a *giambotta*!" This phrase was typically uttered from across the room, and if you heard it, you knew you were being watched. You had better straighten up because someone would be coming in to check up on you. In short, *giambotta* was a model of ambivalence because it could function either as a blessing or a curse. If you had to straighten it out or clean it up, it was a curse. If you could eat it, it was a blessing.

How Not to be Stingy or Greedy: Some Minor Epiphanies

I was not the only pupil who spent extended time in Nannie's kitchen. My cousin Rob also spent many hours watching Nannie cook. Today, I cannot cook a thing, while Rob is an excellent cook, and he has a thriving garden. My father is Rob's godfather, and this spring Rob brought Dad some tomato plants he grew in his own greenhouse. Rob also brought a large basil plant, and he took a clay pot home to start some parsley seeds. While Dad's small garden is now confined to the courtyard of his townhouse, he still describes this little patch of ground as "his garden." My cousin's tender gesture is a way of maintaining continuity between generations and connections between worlds.

Rob and I were reminiscing at a family wedding, and I asked him if he remembered what it felt like to be a child in Nannie's kitchen. A soft light came into his eyes, and in a low tone of voice he said, "Oh yeah." Rob then recalled sitting at the kitchen table, and he held his hands up in one of the characteristic gestures Nannie used while cooking. In Italian, Rob admonished, "*Robertino, no scompardishe!*", and we both started laughing.

These familiar words reflect a larger philosophy of life. In particular, this phrase means do not be skimpy or stingy. While my family may have made this up, I believe that the term is a variation of *scomparire*, which means to make a bad showing, or to disappear. In this case, Nannie was instructing Rob on the importance of not shortchanging ingredients or withholding elements from a recipe. Yet Nannie was also imparting a larger lesson concerning generosity, and how to include as much as needed to produce a good outcome. This lesson is about the balance of largesse, which recognizes the value of the individual elements within one's own creations. In broader terms, this is also about acknowledging the importance of the little luxuries, and the sense of abundance that endows life with extra life.

In my grandparents' world, if you were invited to someone's home for a meal, the food just kept coming, and you were expected to eat everything and enjoy it. Both the experience itself, and the corresponding philosophy of life that it reflected, encompassed the qualities of generosity, hospitality, proportion, skill, care, and abundance. When the meal was over, one of the greatest compliments you could pay the hostess was to say that you were so full, "*Manga no spicchio d'aglio*." This means, "I couldn't eat another clove of garlic." In other words, you stuffed yourself so completely that you couldn't eat another bite; yet the food was so delicious, you ate more than you should have and you had no regrets. "*Manga no spicchio d'aglio*" is a blessing that expresses a paradoxical logic of abundance – somehow, it is too much without being too much. When you heard this phrase, you knew the dinner was a complete success. And of course, none of this could have happened if the hostess was being *scompardishe*.

While being *scompardishe* was one way of going wrong and being out of balance with life, this condition had its counterpart, that of being *scostumato*. While the Italian word literally means to be dissolute or debauched, while I was growing up, people used the term to signify someone who was greedy, a person who took too much and didn't leave enough for others. As a child, this was something you were warned never to do. To illustrate this point, imagine a group of people standing around a dining room table at the end of an anniversary party. It is time to leave, and the host tells the guests to take the leftovers home with them. It goes without saying that all of this homemade Italian food is incredible. While most people will take a small amount of a few items, there is always the person who goes overboard, who gets three paper plates and an entire roll of plastic wrap, and then starts heaping up the goodies. When a person is taking three times as much as they should, they are taking advantage of someone's generosity. This person is being greedy, or *scostumato*.

So to everyone reading this book: *No scompardishe! No scostumato!* Such life lessons are simple and ordinary, yet they are very powerful. The phrases are curses that sit on the other side of blessings. Just as the words convey a larger philosophy of life, they represent a form of vernacular magic. In all cases, the messages are about balance: don't give too little, don't take too much, enjoy life fully, and remember that you can always put something in, but once it is in, you can never take it out again. The effect of such phrases only becomes heightened when the words are expressed in both English and Italian. Then, the concepts assume multiple lives, both literal and metaphorical. When this happens, stories of everyday subjects begin to appear in a new light, like a collection of minor epiphanies – and in a few cases, some major ones.

The Angel Wings at Christmastime

When I asked Dad about his favorite memories of Christmastime, he replied:

They were all good.
My mother would be making something special,
Like the angel wings for Christmas.
I would be outside playing in the back yard,
And she'd call me in

So I could have them.
Family and friends would come
To the house to celebrate,
And even, people who didn't have
Anywhere else to go would be invited.
My mother and father would bend over backwards
To make everything nice for the holidays.

At Christmas, angel wings were always accompanied by traditional Italian honey cookies.

Honey Cookies

Ingredients

1 cup of flour for 2 eggs

Pinch of salt

(Makes about 2 cups, with 4 eggs)

Honey

Directions

Form the dough into rounded or crescent shapes. Fry at moderate heat. Heat honey (not boiling). Use a slotted spoon for frying and honeying.

The Little White Wicker Tree

Both upstairs and downstairs, the living and dining rooms were conjoined by pairs of wooden colonnades. During the holidays, Nannie would place a glass basket filled with Christmas cards in the niche between the columns. She also put a miniature white wicker Christmas tree on the buffet at the side of the dining room table. This tabletop tree matched the furniture in the sun parlor. The little white tree had a white dove perched at the top, and its own special box of fragile, colored glass ornaments. I later learned that the little tree also had its own story. After my grandfather died, Nannie did not have a Christmas tree for several years. Later on, she got the little wicker tree. Once again, this little white tree expresses a paradox of balance. Just as it poignantly reflects the absent presence of my grandfather, it also represents Nannie's ability to reach a state of balance and take joy in life again. As a child, I knew intuitively that the little wicker tree was special, but I didn't know the story. Yet I did know that, when I saw the little tree and the glass basket filled with cards, it was Christmastime.

Another special ornament also has a family history. During the twenties, when Nannie and Grandpa were having the house built, some large trees had to be cut down on the lot. Uncle Henry was a carpenter at a local factory, Stanley Works, and he knew two men from work who came to cut down the trees. These men were always referred to as Goomba Pippie and Goomba Pat. While the title Goomba is generally used in an affectionate, honorary way to connote "Godfather" – with Goomad being the corresponding term for "Godmother" – in this case, the titles were literal. These people became such good friends that Nannie and Grandpa asked Goomba Pippie (whose real name was Joseph) to be Dad's godfather, and his wife, Gooma Rose, to be his godmother.

Even though Goomba Pippie lived a very humble life, one year he brought my father a special Christmas present, a large tabletop ornament with Santa Claus pulling a sleigh. Santa is in his red velvet suit with white fur trim, and the sleigh is pulled by eight reindeer, all standing in glistening white snow. This was a beautiful present, and for many years, the sleigh sat in a place of honor on the living room coffee table. We always referred to it as "Goomba Pippie's sleigh" when it came out at Christmastime.

The Cordials in the Bedroom Closet: My Mother Was Like a Detective

When guests came to visit during the holidays, special candies and cookies would be served, along with coffee and anisette. Dad said that the coffee with anisette was just something the family liked. Accompanying the holiday desserts, there were cordials that resembled miniature parfaits. The bottom portion of a tall crystal shot glass would be filled either with bright green crème de menthe or with clear crème de cacao. The liqueur would then be topped with heavy whipping cream. The cordials were simple yet elegant, and Dad recalls that they were both smooth and festive.

Christmas Candy

Ingredients

Nuts: Almonds and Walnuts

½ pound of sugar for each pound of nuts

Tangerine peel, cut fine

1 drop vanilla

Directions

Bake nuts for 10 minutes at 350 degrees and stir.

Melt sugar and stir, don't burn. Add the ingredients. Stir until firm. Place on wet board and flatten by hand. Wet with cold water or wet rolling pin. Use a wooden spoon and cut as soon as cool enough.

During Prohibition – the national ban on alcohol that extended from 1920 to 1933 – my grandparents kept the bottles of liqueur in a closet in their bedroom. One day, Nannie's father came to visit. Dad's older brother, Uncle Phil (who was also called Uncle Sonny), was just a little boy at the time. After Nannie's father left, Uncle Phil broke out in hives. Nannie called the doctor and the doctor said, "If this were an adult, I would say that this comes from drinking alcohol." Of course, Nannie didn't say anything to the doctor, but it was clear to her exactly what had happened. As Dad said, "She figured it out on her own. My mother was like a detective."

The Arch: A World Within a World

The front of our house faced the street, and it had a sloping green lawn extending up the driveway. The back of the property was fairly extensive, with garages, a patio, and several gardens. The back yard also had a unique decorative structure that allowed you to feel like you were inside and outside at once. This was a large white wooden rose arbor that was always called "the arch." Both upstairs and downstairs, the pantry windows looked directly out onto the arch. On the inside, the arch held two interior benches facing one another. On the overarching exterior lattice, climbing red roses always bloomed around the time of my birthday, on June 1st.

Auntie Theresa, Nannie, Camille, and myself

The photo of Auntie Theresa, Nannie, Camille, and myself, above, was taken in Auntie Theresa's back yard during the summer of 1976. The climbing red roses on the fence are the same type that grew on the arch.

Dad told me the story of the arch. Uncle Henry was a carpenter. He had come to this country from Italy with Grandpa, and he later married one of Nannie's sisters, Aunt Minnie. Uncle Henry lived with my grandparents for a little while, and he made the arch shortly after the house was built in the 1920s. Woodworking was also my father's hobby, and Dad recalled that Uncle Henry did a good job with the construction. As a carpenter, he made the arch by hand with beveled compound angles. In his 70 years of living at the house, Dad rebuilt the arch twice, from scratch. The arch was its own little world – semi-enclosed and semi-open. As a child, I spent countless hours playing inside of it. The arch was like the pantry. From an early point, these transitional spaces showed me that you could be in one world that was located inside of another.

My Grandfather's Fig Tree: It Was the Thing to Do

Tucked in the corner of the vegetable garden was another presence I always knew was special, but I didn't know the story. This was a fig tree that belonged to our grandfather. In my mind, I can still see the distinctive shape of the fig leaves, and feel their fuzzy texture on my fingertips. I can still remember how the green fruits ripened and turned to beautiful shades of mottled eggplant purple. I asked Dad about how the fig tree came to be planted there, and what it had meant to Grandpa:

The fig tree – it was your grandfather's.
He had fig trees,
And they kept dying.
I think it was Uncle Charlie who gave him that tree.
It grew, and it got so big.
It was the only tree that survived.

At that time, a lot of the Italians were getting them.
This climate wasn't meant for them –
Here, we have winters with hard freezes.
So, every year, you'd have to make a hole around it,
And bury it with leaves.
That's what we did.

Sam Costanza also gave him a tree.
I think it came from his garden.
Where you'd bury it, it would sprout other little trees.

Pa gave people parts of the tree.
He'd give them to his friends.
At that time, all of his friends had them.
It was the thing to do.

Nannie didn't cook with figs.
She really didn't have a lot of time for baking,
Although she made an excellent
Pineapple upside-down cake.
She would make the pineapple upside-down cake
For her goomads, when they would come to visit.

If I remember, the figs would come in September.
They'd turn purple, and they'd be red inside.
When you opened them, you'd have to watch
That the ants didn't crawl in.
There was an opening on the bottom
That lent itself to this,
And the ants were attracted by all that sugar.

Oh yeah, Pa liked to eat them.
The biggest crop of figs came
The year your grandfather died.

Looking back at this I realize that, as a child, I was sensing Grandpa's presence as I stood by his tree. This too is a paradoxical story of an absent presence, of continuity and survival, and of people taking their worlds with them.[9] The fig tree is a heritage planting. It tells a larger story of sweetness and survival, of gifts shared within a community, and of the considerable effort that went into keeping

---

[9] Regarding the placement, significance, and careful tending of such fig trees in the gardens of Italian-American families, see Ed Iannuccilli's moving account of "The Fig Tree" in *Growing Up Italian: Grandfather's Fig Tree and Other Stories* (Woonsocket, RI: Barking Cat Books, 2008), pp. 3-5.

everything alive, particularly lives that were lived in multiple worlds.

You Only Have One Family, You Don't Have More

Shortly after he turned 80, I asked Dad what he was proudest of in his life. Without hesitating, he replied, "My family." After mentioning the people in our immediate family, he shifted to a larger perspective:

Where would you be without your family?
Not just the immediate family,
But everyone, the extended family.
That's all family.
People who don't have a family,
If you talk to them,
They're kind of miserable,
And getting into binds all the time,
Because they don't have anyone.

My love of family came from my mother and my father.
Both of them were for the family.
My father was even inviting strangers to the house,
And Nannie would do all that cooking.
One of my friends told me that
He could never remember having anyone
Over in their house,
And that's sad.
Another friend told me they'd never seen
A family like ours.

Family is precious because
You only have one family.
You don't have more.

You'd Just Show Up, and You'd Be Welcomed

In my grandparents' world, the home was part of the community, and the community was part of the home. Both Auntie Theresa and Dad told me that, "Grandpa was famous for inviting people to the house, to eat with us, without letting Nannie know ahead of time. He would bring home an extra two or three people," and Nannie and my aunts would have to cook for them. In those days, not everyone had telephones. If you wanted to visit someone, you wouldn't ask first. You'd just arrive – not at mealtimes, but during the afternoon or evening. As Dad put it, "You wouldn't call ahead. You'd just show up, and you'd be welcomed."

Such qualities of generosity, hospitality, and loyalty were highly valued in this community. As Dad said, "Those people stuck by one another." Sometimes they did so to their own detriment, even occasionally running afoul of the law. Dad told me two such stories of how people demonstrated care for one another, and in so doing, got into trouble with the police. The first story concerns a man my father referred to as Uncle Zizi, who cooked at Nannie and Grandpa's wedding. By trade, this man was a shoemaker, and he had a drinking problem. At one point, people hadn't seen him for a few days, so Uncle Henry went to check on him. This man had hanged himself, and Uncle Henry discovered the body. Uncle Henry cut him down, and then he went to get the police, who reprimanded Uncle Henry. Uncle Henry's act probably was the equivalent of tampering with a crime scene, but he couldn't just leave Uncle Zizi hanging there and walk away. Uncle Henry did what he felt was right, and he adopted a compassionate and ethical approach, even if he was chastised for performing this act.

A different but related incident happened to Grandpa's business partner, Jack Badal. One day Jack was out with the truck that the tailor shop used for deliveries, and Jack saw a man lying in the road. He stopped to pick him up, put him in the truck, and took him to the hospital. By the time they reached the hospital, the man was dead. At the hospital, the police gave Jack a hard time, much as they had with Uncle Henry. Clearly, you can't just show up with a dead body, or lead the police to a corpse, without some sharp questions being asked. Yet even if their actions were technically wrong, both men were acting out of a larger sense of loyalty, dignity, and social responsibility. Both did what they knew in their hearts was right, even if officially, the culture didn't view it that way.

He Was a Marine: Uncle John

Nannie's youngest brother, my great-uncle John, also had a strong ethic of loyalty and sense of service. Uncle John was famous for "just showing up" at Nannie's house, especially at mealtimes, and she would always make something special for him. Because Uncle John visited so often, I got to know him very well. He was a large, gentle, quiet man with a sweet smile, great patience, and a wonderful sense of humor. He was very humble, and he didn't talk very much. Yet once, when I was a teenager, Uncle John told my sister and myself the story of his military service in the Marine Corps during the Second World War.

Uncle John joined the service in the early 1940s. He volunteered to go, and he served for four years. During World War II, Uncle John was assigned to the aircraft carrier the USS *Wasp* when the ship was part of the Pacific Fleet. This was the first time my uncle had ever crossed the ocean, and he told us that the Marines had special names for the guys who were making their first equatorial crossing, as opposed to those who were experienced sailors. He said that the men began as Pollywogs, but that they finished as Shellbacks – and he smiled meaningfully as he said those names. Uncle John was aboard the *Wasp* when it was bombed in 1942; ultimately, the ship was lost in action.

63

After it was hit in battle, part of the ship suffered extensive damage. Uncle John was very lucky to be on the side of the ship that was not hit, so he survived. He told the story so modestly, as if all of this was no big deal, that it was wartime and this was just how things were. Yet as he spoke, a special glow of pride filled his dark brown eyes. I have always been so grateful that he shared this story.

Uncle John loved history, and I know why – because he had lived it. He was a large, burly man and he wore a crew cut. He was kind and soft-spoken, and it was clear that he loved Nannie so much. Yet, Dad told me that Uncle John could be very tough. One time, my uncle returned home from his job as a postman, and he could hear that there was somebody in the house. Uncle John came in through the back door, while the person had broken in through the front door. As Dad tells it: "Your Uncle John sees this guy, and doesn't call the police. Instead, he chased the guy himself, and he even jumped out the window after him. He didn't catch him, which was probably good, because this could have been dangerous." I told Dad I was surprised by this story, because I always remember Uncle John as being so quiet and gentle. Dad laughed and replied, "Yeah, but he was also rugged. You were a little girl. He was a Marine."

Everybody Would Always Win Something

Until Grandpa sold the tailor shop, he was working all hours at the business. During this time, one of Grandpa's favorite forms of recreation was playing cards with his friends. He belonged to a club for Italian-American men. Every Sunday, Grandpa would leave the house between two and three in the afternoon, and he wouldn't return home until nine o'clock at night. Dad said that Grandpa needed the relaxation because he worked so hard during the week. At the club, they didn't gamble for money, because Grandpa didn't like that. Instead, those who liked to drink would translate their winnings into drinks. Grandpa didn't drink, but he would get a box of candy, or a bag of candy bars, and bring them home to the family.

For their first real vacation, Nannie and Grandpa rented a large corner cottage at Sound View Beach, on Hartford Avenue in Old Lyme, Connecticut. The family took a two-week vacation on the water. While Dad's family stayed in the cottage, at various times, relatives and friends would come to visit. Dad was ten that summer, and he remembered the day a group of cousins arrived. "They drove a coupe, and there were more people than they could get into the car. So, some rode in the car, and the rest went all the way to the beach holding onto the running boards. It took 35 to 40 minutes to get there, so this was a long way."

Another group of family members rented a nearby cottage for one week, and then Dad was able to play with his cousin, Sonny Nesta, who was Uncle Rockie and Aunt Mary from Hartford's son. From the cottages, it was about a ten-minute walk to the water. As a little boy, Dad would continually run in and out of the water, and the insteps of his feet got so badly sunburned that they blistered. Dad's cousin was only a few years older, but he took care of him. "It was Sonny Nesta who saved me. He put me in a chair and moved me around to where he'd want me. He did this until I got better and I could walk again." Even as children, these people took care of one another.

We Would Have a Banquet

Before Grandpa sold the tailor shop, the family would take day trips during the summertime. On Sundays, they would go to Hammonasset Beach State Park in Madison, Connecticut. As my father vividly recalled:

We did this on many Sundays during the summer.
That was our vacation.
We used to eat at the pavilion.

We would place a cloth tablecloth
On the picnic table on the pavilion,
And my mother and sisters would set the picnic table
Like it was a real table,
With the tablecloth, but with paper plates and cups.
Nannie would make these wonderful meals
Of stuffed rice.
This was her specialty, so we would have that for lunch.
Gooma Rose's specialty was roasted chicken,
And that would be there, too.

But, your Auntie Bea didn't like it.
We'd have a banquet,
And the Americans would have little white sandwiches
Wrapped in wax paper
That they carried in little picnic baskets.

At our table, the men would keep the beer cold
By getting a five-gallon pail –
The kind contractors would use –
Going to the icehouse, and filling the pail with ice.
As the day went on, the water would melt.
One time, at the end of the day,
Goomba Pippie went to dump the water out,
And he hit people with melted ice water,
And he soaked them!
The funny part is, these people only lived
On the next street over.

Goomba Pippie would always bring homemade wine
To these picnics,
And Gooma Rose would always bring a roasted chicken.
We'd have all this stuff to carry.
Goomba Pippie would put all these things
In a bushel basket, with a wire handle.
Your Auntie Bea hated having to help
Carry these items back and forth,

From the car to the pavilion,
And back to the car.
It was a full dinner at the beach.
The "Americans" your Auntie Bea admired
Would only have these crummy little
White bread sandwiches.
But, we would have a feast.

This poignant story expresses a classic tension between traditional cultural values and the contrasting desires for independence and assimilation associated with members of a younger generation. This ambivalent story also shows how people felt either cursed or blessed by the worlds they did (or did not) belong to. There is something so distinctly funny – and so very typical – about how Goomba Pippie had to travel over 30 miles to accidentally fling melted ice water on the American neighbors who only lived one street over. People cannot help but be themselves, and all of these stories are true to character.

While growing up, I always admired Auntie Bea because she had such a strong personality. She was so outgoing and spirited and independent. In contrast, even as a young child, Dad's core values were very conservative and traditional. Even though these events occurred more than 70 years ago, Dad still has trouble understanding his older sister's perspective. To this day, he laughs out loud when he thinks of how anyone could ever be envious of "the Americans" who only had their "crummy little white sandwiches", while just a few feet away, "We had it good. We had a feast."

Nannie's Stuffed Rice

Ingredients

Sauce

Small meatballs

Sausage

2 or 3 hardboiled eggs

Partially cooked rice

Grated cheese

Provolone

Mozzarella

1 or 2 eggs, beaten, for the top

Directions

Layer of sauce with grated cheese, layer of rice, layer of meat, layer of egg, layer of rice. More grated cheese, provolone and mozzarella, layer of sauce.

Bake at 400 degrees for about 20 minutes, then pour on beaten egg until set. Bake uncovered.

She Would Always Have Something Good For Us

The family vacation days did not begin or end at the beach. As Auntie Theresa reminded Dad, when the family was going to Hammonasset, they would stop first at Goomba Pippie and Gooma Rose's house. Goomba Pippie didn't drive, but their house was on the way, so Grandpa would pick them up. Auntie Theresa recalled that, on those days, "Gooma Rose would always have something good for us." Hearing this, I thought she meant that Gooma Rose would contribute to the food that the families shared at the beach. Yet the feasting neither began nor ended there. When I asked Dad if Auntie Theresa had meant that Gooma Rose would occasionally provide a special treat, he emphatically replied: "No! We'd eat all day long!" There was always an abundance of good things, and the feasting went on all day.

After an elaborate noon dinner, the children would play on the beach, the men would go off to play cards, and the women would drink coffee on the pavilion and visit together. Then it would be supper time, and the family would either have cookout-style food, or they would get sandwiches at a little restaurant nearby. When it came time to drive home, they would reverse their route and drop off Gooma Rose and Goomba Pippie first. Then there would be the third feast of the day, which consisted of an elaborate dessert and coffee. Gooma Rose would put out Italian cookies, or specialty cookies she made, some of which were called "Chinese Chews." Because Dad liked these cookies so much, my mother got the recipe from Gooma Rose:

Gooma Rose's Chinese Chews

Ingredients

½ cup of margarine (1 stick)

1 cup sugar

3 well-beaten eggs

1 cup flour

½ teaspoon salt

1 cup dates

1 cup nuts (walnuts)

1 teaspoon vanilla

Directions

Cream the butter, add sugar, and mix; add well-beaten eggs, flour, salt, and mix well. Add dates, nuts, and vanilla. Grease a square baking pan and pour in. Bake at 350 degrees for 25 minutes. When cool, cut into strips and sprinkle with confectioner's sugar.

Even when they were both in their eighties, Dad and Auntie Theresa remembered these outings vividly. In their feasts at the beach, even the smallest details of life could appear like miniature works of art. These scenes are magical because they show this world at its best. The stories tell of hospitality and homemaking, and of how we never forget what we learn as children. In their youth, Dad and Auntie Theresa were taught how to create something good, and how powerful it was to have good things to share with others. This is a family love story, a tale of *agape*, a feast of love that exemplifies how our grandparents created a world, and how they took that world with them, wherever they went.

Coda: Having Tea with Transcendence

Several years ago, my husband and I were walking in a large antique shop in Houston, and I came across a little china creamer. It was an odd piece that had gone astray from a larger set. With its gilt edges, its delicate white body, and its interlaced wreaths of pink and blue flowers, I recognized it at once as part of the Pope Gosser "Blue Bell" pattern, and thus, as the same pattern as Nannie's everyday china. These dishes were always kept in the pantry, and Nannie used them all the time.

The creamer in the same pattern as Nannie's everyday china

When I saw the little creamer in the antique store, I vividly remembered numerous childhood afternoons, even as I returned to the ever-present moment. And once again, I saw my life become multiple. Much like the interlaced garlands of flowers that decorate the creamer, many times, places, and presences were all interwoven with one another.

In the world our grandparents created, home and family *were* sacred. Thus, in so many ways, the little creamer sits on the windowsill, perched between the sacred and the profane. It is so modest, yet it is so powerful. It is so small, yet it is so large. We never forget what we learn as children. I recognize the pattern and, as I sit with the creamer, once again, I'm having tea with transcendence.

IV

I THINK WE WOULD KNOW IF THE BED WAS ON FIRE: MY PARENTS' GENERATION

The Shoe-Make

Nannie's seven children were all born at home. Six of the children lived well into adulthood, and five lived either just shy of, or well past, their 80th birthdays. The first five children were born at the block, where Nannie was attended by a midwife. The two youngest, Auntie Theresa and my father, were born in the house I grew up in, and they were delivered by the family doctor. The stories of the births are associated with both curses and blessings.

When Nannie and Grandpa were first married, the Italian-American doctor who served their neighborhood was very gruff, and he lacked a bedside manner. While this doctor had received his medical degree from Yale University, in the neighborhood he was known as "The Shoe-Make". This was not because of his poor medical skills, but because he treated people like they were objects. When Nannie was having her first child, she told my grandfather, "I don't want the Italian doctor," and she saw another doctor instead. When the time came for the baby to be born, Grandpa and Uncle Angelo walked downtown to get Nannie's doctor. That doctor said he had a bad head cold and he wasn't coming out. Uncle Angelo said to Grandpa, "She has no choice," and they went to get the Italian doctor. Hearing of the situation, the doctor replied in frustration, "Those darn Italian women never see a doctor until the baby is ready to be born, and then they get me!" By the time they returned home, the baby had arrived.

Dad likes to contrast this story with that of his own birth. My father was delivered by the family doctor, whom everyone adored. When Grandpa called the doctor to tell him that the new baby was coming, the doctor was in the next town over. This was in 1936, and the doctor made the trip from Hartford to New Britain in 12 minutes flat. As Dad said, "This is how that doctor took care of us."

On several occasions in our family, the blessings of good care were associated with the curses of serious illnesses or accidents. As a child, I often heard allusions to the time Nannie "went over the railing." Yet I was never quite sure what this meant, so I asked Dad. He told me that, until he and my mother were married, the family lived on the first floor of the three-story house, where there was an open back porch with a clothesline. Nannie was not a tall woman, and she had to stand on a little stool in order to reach the line. One time, when she reached for it, the cord snapped. Instead of letting go of the rope, she held on, and the line took her with it, slamming her into a concrete wall. The impact compressed Nannie's fifth vertebra. This occurred in 1948, when Dad was 12 years old.

There was no surgery, but Nannie was hospitalized for five weeks. The orthopedic doctor initially placed Nannie in a level position in a hospital bed, with the head and the foot of the bed reversed. Over the next several weeks, the angle of inclination was gradually increased, until the vertebra opened and function returned. At the hospital, Nannie was attended by the orthopedic specialist, but the family doctor saw her every day, as well. When it came time for her to return home, the family doctor accepted no payment for his services. While Nannie wore a back brace for some time afterwards, she was ultimately able to discard it. The orthopedic doctor initially told Grandpa that Nannie would be an invalid, and Dad still recalls being frightened by this news. As he said, "It took a long time, but your grandmother recovered. Two of your aunts worked in factory offices at the time, but they were allowed to work different hours, so that one of them could always be at home, taking care of your grandmother."

My grandparents' world was characterized by such a communal ethic of caregiving. During the 1920s, one of Nannie's younger brothers developed a serious infection, and he needed surgery. They set up a miniature operating room in the family house, and the doctor performed the procedure there. As Dad said, "He did a good job. Nannie's friend Marie went over and assisted the doctor, even though she wasn't actually a nurse. Those people helped each other out."

Such early-twentieth-century healthcare stories demonstrate the various ways in which people took care of one another, or how they failed to do so. Even with the Italian-American doctor's excellent education, people still saw and described him as being the opposite of a good practitioner, hence his nickname, "The Shoe-Make." This term was like a professional curse that followed him around throughout his career. The label implied not just shoddy work, but someone who made people feel uncared for, especially when they were at their most vulnerable. Ironically, one of the best-credentialed professionals in the community was perpetually known as his opposite. Yet the family doctor who showed great care and compassion was always spoken of affectionately. Everyone loved him, and they felt his presence was a blessing.

In That Same Bedroom

The home was the center of the most intimate aspects of life, including birth, death, and marriage. Dad recalled that, as a young man, he always slept very soundly. One night, he was woken out of his sleep because he heard a loud noise in the bathroom. He got up to see what was happening, and he found Grandpa in the bathroom with Nannie. Grandpa had been battling metastatic intestinal cancer, and he had made it from the bedroom to the bathroom, and he passed away there. Even though my father was of a slender build, that night he got the kind of brute strength people get during emergencies. Dad lifted Grandpa up, "like he was a baby," took him in his arms, and put him back into bed. This was the same bedroom that my father and mother shared during the 40 years of married life they spent together in that house. This was the same bedroom where Auntie Theresa and Dad had been born.

After my father's birth, a family friend came to stay with Nannie for several days. This woman was Gooma Leen's sister-in-law. While not related by blood, the families were so close that Gooma Leen became Auntie Bea's godmother, just as Goomba Pippie and Gooma Rose were Dad's godfather and godmother. When my father was christened, a very special guest attended the party, and this too was a blessing. In our town, there was another man whose last name was also Gagliardi. The families were not related, as this man came from a different part of Italy. Yet, he and my grandfather knew each other. During the thirties, this man's son was a well-known opera singer, and he had performed at the Metropolitan Opera in New York. Grandpa persuaded the man to have his son sing at my father's christening. As Dad said, "How my father got him to sing there, I don't know. It wasn't at the church. It was at the party at the house, after the ceremony."

The Diamond and the Bicycle

Dad's two oldest sisters, Auntie Palma and Auntie Bea, had extremely different temperaments. Yet, they were very good friends, and they traveled together socially. Both women collected antiques, and their homes were beautiful. Auntie Palma was the oldest sibling, and she was very reserved and gentle, quiet and ladylike. Auntie Bea was the next oldest, and she was very outgoing and social, progressive and adventurous. In short, my two aunts complemented one another wonderfully. Like so many members of the family, Auntie Bea had the gift of hospitality, and she would host lovely gatherings. Auntie Palma always said that "Bea had the knack. She could put a few crackers on a plate and make it look like a banquet."

Auntie Palma was exceptionally kind and good to everyone. As Dad put it, "She would rather hurt herself than anyone else." Dad recalls the time that, as a young woman, Auntie Palma was riding a bicycle in the back yard. Portions of our back yard were quite steep and hilly. As she was riding, the bicycle spun out of control and started going down the driveway, and then down the sloping embankment of the lawn. Ultimately, Auntie Palma landed at the bottom of the hill, in our next-door neighbor's yard, by their cellar door. Thankfully, she did not fall or get hurt. While all of this was happening, Auntie Palma's concern was not for herself. She had recently become engaged, and her fiancé had given her a diamond ring. Auntie Palma's concern was that she didn't want to hit the diamond on the side of the house after she went down the hill.

This story illustrates the importance of balance, in every sense of the word. The narrative conveys the lesson that it is necessary to value yourself as much as you value other people and material objects. Part of living in balance means there are times when we have to stand our ground, both literally and metaphorically. Dad remembers one evening when Auntie Palma rose to the occasion. She had just cleaned up the kitchen after dinner, and her husband wanted her to make something else. As Dad said, "This was not at all like Palma, but she said, 'No, the kitchen's closed.'" And Dad said, "'Bravo Palma!' This was not like her, and I was glad she stuck to it." Many years later, he still remembers the stories of how the siblings loved and supported each other, especially when it came to setting boundaries.

Auntie Palma was also superstitious. Both she and Nannie thought that it brought good luck to eat lentil soup on New Year's Day, so they subscribed to this Italian custom. Hearing this, I smiled and asked Dad if any other vegetable soup was also considered lucky, perhaps *pastaefagiole*? He laughed and said, "No – *pastaefagiole* isn't lucky, but you were lucky if you got some, because it filled your stomach."

Lentil Soup

Ingredients

½ package of lentil beans

1 carrot

1 celery

½ onion

Celery salt

Regular salt

Pepper

Approximately ¼ cup olive oil

1 large soup spoon of tomato (optional)

Directions

Check over the lentil beans and wash them thoroughly. Dice the celery, carrot, and onions. Put the beans into ½ pan of fresh water. Add other ingredients. Cook for about one hour. When it begins to boil, lower the flame. Taste in one hour. Turn off when cooked.

Pastaefagiole

Directions

Fry out garlic in oil. When brown, remove garlic. Add beans which have been rinsed in cold water. Add water to cover beans. Season with salt and pepper. Pour in one heaping cupful of ditalini. Cook macaroni partially. Add to bean mixture and cook until macaroni is done and cooked to taste. Cover when cool.

The Companion Salt Dishes

After Auntie Palma passed away, her son Gene gifted various family members with some of her belongings, as keepsakes. I received one of the small crystal salt dishes that Auntie Palma kept on a special shelf in her wainscoted dining room, and which she used during formal dinners at her home. Several years later, Auntie Bea passed away. Her son John similarly gifted family members with antiques from Auntie Bea's house, so that they would have something to remember her by. I was thrilled to receive one of Auntie Bea's small glass salt dishes. I keep the two salt dishes together on a table in my living room. When I look at them, it's as though the two sisters are traveling together in spirit, much as they did in life.

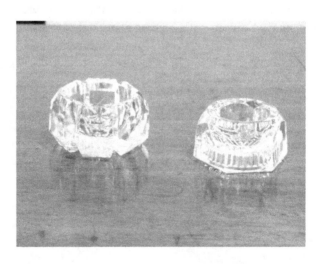

Auntie Palma's salt dish is on the left,
Auntie Bea's is on the right

Dad told me that, when they were growing up, Auntie Bea and their next oldest sister, Auntie Florie, used to argue like crazy – but they always did this when they were alone, and *never in front of Nannie*. Auntie Bea was very independent and oriented toward the outer world, whereas my other aunts were more domestic and inwardly-focused. From the time she was a girl, Auntie Bea was far less interested in housework than in social interactions. The third floor of the house was rented out to another family, and Dad recalled that "Your Auntie Bea would go up to visit them at dish time." Auntie Florie understandably got very tired of this, so she went into the back hall and called up two full flights of stairs, "Bea – telephone!" When Auntie Bea came down and asked, "Where's my call?" Auntie Florie replied, "Help with the dishes!" Everyone laughed, and Dad remembers that they laughed even harder when Auntie Bea responded, "I fail to see the humor in this!"

Like Auntie Bea, Uncle Henry's wife, Aunt Minnie, also "wasn't the most ambitious" when it came to domestic tasks. Dad recalls that, one time, she had a big stack of dishes in her hands, and while she was washing them, they fell and she dropped them. The women made a joke of this, telling Aunt Minnie, "You dropped them so that you wouldn't have to wash them!" Of course, she said she didn't. Aunt Minnie was also a great cook, and my mother's recipe box contains a notecard for...

Pork Chops à la Aunt Minnie

Directions

Season and brown pork chops. Put 1 cup rice on pork chops. Add green peppers and onions, sliced thin (optional). Next add tomatoes, mashed up, or add tomato sauce. Sprinkle a little oregano and garlic salt. If dry, add water. Bake at 400 degrees for 1 ½ hours.

Would It Be Alright If I Gave You Some Ravioli?

While I was growing up, I spent a great deal of time in Auntie Florie's house. Much like Nannie, Auntie Florie was a creative artist with food, and both of their kitchens were absolutely magical. Auntie Florie was more modern than Nannie, and her home had a slightly different atmosphere. While Nannie's recipes were traditional, Auntie Florie had a broader repertoire, and she was a master baker, cook, and chef. Her homemade bread was *legendary* – it was perfectly formed and light as a feather. One Easter, she invited our family to dinner, and she served Beef Wellington for the main course. On another occasion, she made an amazing dinner of coconut-crusted, beer-battered shrimp. You really had to have seen all of this to believe it. And, even if you were there, Auntie Florie's desserts were even more unbelievable. While she would make elaborate cakes and other exotic creations, my favorite was a traditional light yellow sponge cake filled and covered with her own homemade butter fudge frosting. There is no way to overstate how marvelous this was. Just ask anyone in the family about Auntie Florie's cooking...

Yet my favorite dish of all was Auntie Florie's (and Nannie's) traditional homemade chicken soup with pastene, which are tiny dots of pasta. Auntie Florie sometimes put escarole in the broth, but Nannie did not do this.

Chicken Soup with Pastene

Directions

Wash a whole chicken, and soak it in a clean dishpan in saltwater. After it's well soaked, boil the chicken for about an hour, until the meat is so tender that it comes off the bones. Our family only made this soup with minimal amounts of vegetables, so they would cook a few pieces of carrots and celery and add them to the broth. Fresh Italian parsley would also be added, and it too would cook in the broth and become soft. Add salt to taste. In a separate pan, boil hot water and cook pastene until tender, and then pour into the chicken broth. Dad said that the package for these small pasta beads says *acini di pepe*, not pastene, but I remember this pasta always being called pastene. The soup would be served with freshly grated parmesan cheese as a garnish.

In addition to her exquisite cooking, Auntie Florie was known for her sense of humor. She had the personality of a trickster, or as Dad put it, "She had the devil in her. Just like Pa." Much like Grandpa, Auntie Florie would make candid statements that would unbalance the status quo. As you'll see, these slightly nonsensical comments would convey the truth while turning everything on its head. Like cooking, humor is a gift, and Auntie Florie was a master. While she was certainly a modest person, Auntie Florie was also honest enough to realize just how much everyone *loved* her cooking, and she was spunky enough to make jokes about this. When someone would visit her house, they would not only be treated to a feast, but they would not leave empty-handed. Containers would be packed up to "tide you over" for the next several days. When Auntie Florie's two domains of cooking and humor converged, it looked something like this:

Auntie Florie would look innocently into your eyes and smile a big smile. She would adopt a very clear and distinct tone of voice, as if she were speaking to someone who was not too bright, or who didn't speak English, or both. Then she would slowly ask: "Would it be alright if I gave you some *rav-i-ol-i*?" It was as though she was asking you for permission, and that you were doing her a monumental favor by taking it off her hands. Obviously, no one would ever say no. After asking her 'innocent' question, Auntie Florie wouldn't wait around for an answer. She would chuckle and head off to the kitchen, and she'd start packing up the containers to go.

Manicotti

Directions

Mix together: Ricotta, mozzarella or provolone, parsley, some salt, 1 beaten egg, and grated parmesan cheese.

Parboil lasagna strips. Cut in half. Fill with the mixture, and roll like braciole. Place in pan and cover with sauce. Cover with foil. Bake at 400 degrees for ½ hour, then uncover.

That Girl Would Rather Have Soup Than a Steak

After I graduated from college, my husband and I lived in suburban Boston. During the summertime, I would host day trips for my family to Boston's North End, which is the Italian section of town.

One day, we were all at a North End restaurant, seated together for lunch at a single long table. Everyone was ordering traditional Italian dishes for their "main meal." I ordered what I truly wanted – a large bowl of escarole soup. It came with homemade bread, and I was thrilled when I saw it on the menu. When the food arrived, everyone looked over at me and, as usual, they were concerned I wasn't getting enough to eat. First, they threw dirty looks at my bowl of escarole soup. Then they whipped out their bread plates and started heaping substantial portions of their own meals onto the smaller dishes. In another moment, an entire flotilla of Italian food would be heading down the long table, making its way directly at me. While everyone meant well, this definitely felt overwhelming, and I started getting concerned. (Just what the hell was I going to do with all that Italian food?!) In real-time, Auntie Florie saw what was happening, and she decided to put an end to the nonsense. She looked straight up and down the expanse of the long table and said in a loud, clear voice, "That girl would rather have soup than a steak!"

As if on cue, everyone nodded and agreed, and they resigned themselves to the inevitable. A pronouncement had been made, a truth had been declared, and the conversation moved on. Thank goodness. And thank you, Auntie Florie, for coming to my rescue. At that time, I was a married woman in my early thirties, with a Ph.D., teaching at a university. Of course, none of that mattered. I was still "that girl" who always sat quietly on Nannie's footstool or in the corner of the kitchen, watching everyone and everything, and never forgetting anything.

They Had the Devil In Them

Auntie Florie loved to tease people. As children, Auntie Theresa and Dad would get silly over things Auntie Florie would do, and then they would get scolded – but of course, they were not the root of the trouble. Auntie Theresa's favorite example of this is known as "the creamed carrots."

One of Grandpa's friends was named Goomba Andy. Despite his first name, Auntie Theresa insisted that "this man was extremely Italian." He was Uncle Pippie's goomba, and one day my grandfather brought the man home for dinner. Knowing that this was a non sequitur, Auntie Florie went right up to where they were sitting and asked, in an innocent voice, "Uncle Andy, do you like *creamed carrots*?" As Auntie Theresa clearly recalled, "Of course, he had no idea what she was asking, and he said in incomprehension, in a thick Italian accent, *'Creamed carrots*?'" Then Auntie Florie ran away, laughing. Dad and Auntie Theresa saw the whole thing, and of course, they thought it was really funny. They started laughing, and while they were being scolded by Nannie, Auntie Florie was nowhere to be seen. This incident became a metaphor for a certain type of mischief. To do a "creamed carrots" meant to set up a prank, spring the trap, and then run away laughing while leaving your younger siblings to take the fall.

Uncle Andy was not the only target of Auntie Florie's sense of humor. According to Dad, so was Goomba Pippie. Goomba Pippie was "not the most ambitious person. He wasn't in love with working, but he worked because he had to." Dad recalled that, when he got off of work, the first thing Goomba Pippie would do was to look for a five-gallon pail, turn it upside down, and sit down on it. Later in life, he worked as a high school custodian; the joke was that it took him a whole day to change a roll of toilet paper, and that doing this job gave him blisters. When someone congratulated him on having a lifetime job in the public school system, Goomba Pippie replied, "Yeah, it's a lifetime job. You never stop working."

One day, Goomba Pippie was in my grandparents' dining room, and Auntie Florie walked up to him and asked, in a serious tone of voice, "Goomba Pippie, do you work too hard?" He immediately replied, "No!" He grabbed a spoon from the dining room table and moved it over a few inches. He said, "If this spoon has to be moved from here to here, I tell Rose to do it." You all know what happens next. Everyone starts laughing, Auntie Florie quickly disappears, and Dad and Auntie Theresa get scolded when Nannie returns to the dining room.

Dad insists that Auntie Florie inherited this sense of humor from Grandpa. In his shops, Grandpa would say things in Italian to difficult people, knowing that they would not understand – but that my father *would*, and it would make him silly. As Dad recalled, "Your grandfather had the devil in him. Auntie Florie had it too. So did Uncle Sonny."

Ladies First

When I asked Dad just what he meant by "Grandpa had the devil in him," he shared some more stories:

When your grandfather was tailoring,
There was a man who would come into the shop,
To help out and run errands.
Grandpa and his partner were devilish.
One day, they told this guy that
The pressing machine was running out of steam.
They gave him a metal pail and twenty-five cents,
And they sent him down the street
To go buy a pail of steam.

Hearing this, I said, "Yes, but the man knew they were joking, right?" And Dad said, "No! He went down the street to go buy a pail of steam." Dad also recalled:

One night we were at Aunt Lucy's.
There were a lot of people at the dining room table.
It was nighttime, and we were having coffee.
The table was loaded with people,
And they were passing cups of coffee all around.
My father picked up a cup of coffee,
And he said, "Ladies first."
Then he turned to Nannie's brother and said,
"Here Charlie, here's a cup for you."

He Was a Brother

While Uncle Sonny was the next oldest sibling, he was not the first boy to be born in the family. Nannie and Grandpa had an infant son, Felice, who died suddenly when he was only three weeks old. This child was named for Grandpa's father in Italy. After he passed away, they gave Uncle Sonny a related name, Felix (although everyone always called him Phil, or Sonny). Nannie's father was named Alfonse, and my father's first name is Alfred, which is a variation on the name of his maternal grandfather. In turn, my sister Camille is named for my grandfather, Camillo.

While I was growing up, Nannie would occasionally mention "the baby who died." From a young age, I was aware of this very tender, absent presence – and of the paradox of a life that was differently present within the life of my family. Dad specifically asked me to include Felice in this book. As he movingly said, "You might want to put him in. He was a brother."

The Mayor of Arch Street

In some ways, Uncle Sonny was a lot like Uncle John – a large, stocky man who could be gruff and tough with people, but who was always so kind and gentle with my sister and me. Uncle Sonny inherited my grandparents' package store after Grandpa retired. As children, he spoiled us – he let us drink as much soda as we could hold from the cooler by the side of the counter. Once, when I was 11, a relative scolded me for something at a family party, and I went to my room, crying. Uncle Sonny witnessed the whole thing, and he came right in after me. He told me not to feel bad, and he spoke in such a gentle and understanding way that we were all back in the living room a short time later.

Unlike Uncle John, Uncle Sonny had a wicked sense of humor, and he could be something of a wise guy. My grandparents' block was located on Arch Street and, because Uncle Sonny spent so much of his life in this location, he was affectionately known as "The Mayor of Arch Street."

Uncle Sonny was gifted with hospitality, with mechanical things, and with running small businesses. When he was 16, Uncle Sonny decided he didn't want to attend high school any longer. Nannie told him the only way he could stop was if he learned a trade, so that's what he did. My uncle applied for a job at a tool and die company. When the manager called to check on the application, Nannie said that her son could only leave school if he learned a trade. The manager took this as a sign of permission, so he hired my uncle. Uncle Sonny put in four years at the local machine shop, he learned the trade, and then he was almost immediately drafted into the Army. He never did work as a tool and die maker. Before he left for the Army, Uncle Sonny took all of his toolboxes, locked them up tightly, and put them in the attic of Nannie's family home because it was dry there, and they would not rust. "And you know how long those toolboxes sat there, unopened?" Dad asked me, "Between 30 and 35 years."

When Uncle Sonny came out of the Army, he went to trade school for auto mechanics under the G.I. Bill, and then he worked at a local garage. As Dad observed, "The place wasn't large, but this garage put engines into cars, and into the delivery trucks that the factories would use. He apprenticed there, and he also went to trade school to learn the 'book part' of the job. So, he learned that trade, too." After doing this work for a while, my uncle worked as a service man for the local gas company. Then, when my grandfather retired, Uncle Sonny ran the package store for several decades. When he could have retired, Uncle Sonny chose to do something else instead – he opened a shoemaker shop in a storefront on the first floor of the block, right next to where my grandfather's tailor shop had been. No one had ever taught Uncle Sonny the trade. It just came to him naturally, like so many things he learned while observing people, all his life.

The Top of the Arch

While reminiscing about his siblings, Dad shared a classic childhood story about Uncle Sonny and Auntie Theresa:

I wasn't old enough at the time,
But when Sonny was old enough,
He got the job of painting the arch.
He decided it would be easier to climb on top to paint,
Rather than use the ladder.
So he climbed on top of the arch,
And he took the paint can with him.
The nails were old and rusty,
And they broke loose and the wood gave way.

Sonny went right through the top of the arch,
And the bucket of white paint went with him,
And it went all over him.
He looked like a snowman.

Fortunately, he didn't get hurt.
He called out to Theresa,
And together, they got him cleaned up.
He would always go to her when there was a problem.
She always helped him out.

While everyone always went to Auntie Theresa, she and my father were especially close. We are fortunate to have two pictures of my father and Auntie Theresa together. The top photo dates from the mid-1940s, and the bottom one was taken 60 years later, at a family wedding. Their strong bond is evident in both portraits.

Dad and Auntie Theresa, mid-1940s

Auntie Theresa and Dad, 2016

Stay For a Quick Cup of Coffee

Because Auntie Theresa's house was only one block away from ours, Ginnie, Camille, and I often played together as children. When I was little, I thought the seven most beautiful words in the English language were: "Stay for a quick cup of coffee." Of course, these words were not directed at me. Instead, they were what Auntie Theresa always said to my mother right after Mom told us to go get our coats because it was time to go home. My mother loved black coffee, and she would almost always give in and stay for one more cup, which meant we had a little extra playtime.

Ginnie would make up all sorts of imaginative games. One of our favorites was called "Stuck in the Car." We would play this downstairs in the finished basement of Auntie Theresa's bungalow home. Even though this area was technically a basement, it was furnished like a miniature apartment, and *everything was immaculate and sparkling clean*. Dare I say it? You could have eaten off the floor! Because this was also a quiet place where we could jump around and make noise, Auntie Theresa let us play there on one condition, namely: "Don't make dust!" Ginnie and I would giggle over that phrase. Obviously, Auntie Theresa was telling us not to be disorderly or make a mess. But we always took the phrase literally, and we asked each other how it was possible for three girls "to make dust." Somehow, this seemed like an act of divine creation, like something only God could do.

During these years, Auntie Theresa drove a large, cream-colored station wagon that was affectionately known as Bessie. She would use this vehicle to go grocery shopping, to take us to school, to run errands, and to take us out for treats. In Connecticut, we experienced hard winters with several feet of snow. Thus, the underlying premise of "Stuck in the Car" was that Ginnie, Camille, and I were out running errands and a snowstorm suddenly struck. Somehow, we would have just gone grocery shopping and picked up clothes at the cleaners, so we magically had all that we needed for sustenance and survival as the storm hit. For props, we used cans of food that Auntie Theresa stored in the basement cupboards. Ginnie would set these items up as though they were in grocery bags on the back seat of the car. We even had an ironing board back there! What were we thinking? Perhaps, we could do a little extra laundry in our spare time? Even as children traveling together in an imaginary station wagon during an imaginary snowstorm: *No Sporcaccione!*

"Stuck in the Car" was a creative fusion of fantasy and reality. Even as a pretend blizzard raged outside, we were having a great time inside. In this space of safety and confinement, we were creating a world all our own, and we were taking this world with us as we hit the imaginary road. Upstairs, my mother stayed for a quick cup of coffee, while downstairs, we had food, clothing, and shelter. We had everything we needed. We laughed and played together, and we had each other.

I Think We Would Know If the Bed Was On Fire

Shortly after Auntie Florie passed away, Auntie Theresa told me a story that is absolutely priceless. Before I even begin, there are two key points to keep in mind. First, none of my aunts were physically large or tall women. Like Dad, Auntie Theresa was of a very slender build, while Auntie Florie was diminutive in stature, like Nannie. Second, everything in these homes was not just clean, *it was immaculate*, and it didn't get that way on its own. While these women were tiny, this did not stop them from being dynamos. As Auntie Theresa used to say, "You were like a one-man army. You had to be!"

One day, Auntie Florie decided to clean her and Uncle George's bedroom. This meant that Auntie Florie took the entire room apart, including stripping the bed and lifting the mattress up off the box spring to air it out. Somehow, in the process of flipping the mattress over, the top of the mattress grazed the switch of an overhead lamp, and it turned the light on. Not realizing what had just happened, Auntie Florie propped the mattress up against the light fixture and walked away. When I asked Dad to confirm Auntie Theresa's story, he said that it was all true, but he insisted on taking a no-fault approach to the situation. He firmly emphasized: "Auntie Florie didn't turn the light on. The mattress turned the light on." (Of course, how could I be so silly? It was the *mattress* that turned the light on, not *Auntie Florie*. Oh, how those people stuck together.)

Back in the bedroom, the lamp gave off so much heat that the mattress caught fire from the contact. Seeing that the bed was on fire, does Auntie Florie call the local fire department? Oh no, an even better idea comes to mind. She decides to call Auntie Theresa, instead. While Auntie Theresa's house was on the other side of town – and thus, at quite a distance from Auntie Florie's – these practical details in no way stopped them. Auntie Theresa got into the car and drove right over to help Auntie Florie put out the fire and repair the damage to the scorched mattress. Once again, this story shows how the siblings supported one another in all circumstances – especially if the job required the efforts of a two-woman army.

Auntie Theresa told me this story when she was in her mid-eighties. At the time, she was grappling with a difficult cancer diagnosis. Her oncologist had put her on a new medication to treat multiple myeloma, and she was very concerned about the drug's potential side effects. There were various phone numbers she was supposed to call if she experienced one symptom or another. One of her primary concerns was that she could be experiencing one of these distressing conditions and not fully realize it. We discussed everything for quite a while, and I told her not to worry, that she would certainly know if and when she needed medical help. Later that afternoon, I made a card for her:

Dear Auntie Theresa,

I think we would know if the bed

was on fire

Much love, Marcia

Pistachio

While she was a very quiet and modest person, compared to my dad, Auntie Theresa was downright adventurous. She had a wonderful flair for living. When I was little, my parents would often serve ice cream for dessert after dinner. Yet the ice cream flavors were always the same. The cartons either held vanilla, or three patchwork sections containing vanilla, chocolate, and strawberry. As a child, I thought that ice cream only came in these flavors. To my delight, I learned that this was wrong information.

During the summer I turned six, Ginnie, Camille, and I were out shopping with Auntie Theresa. It was a warm afternoon, and she took us to a local ice cream shop for a treat. When she went to the booth, to order her cone, I distinctly heard her utter the word "pistachio," and a lightbulb went off in my head. A minute later, when the waitress passed the cone through the window, my aunt's ice cream was bright green like a vegetable, but it tasted sweet, like a dessert. This blew my mind – and not only because I had just discovered the wonders of pistachio ice cream. This experience taught me that there were more options available in life than just plain vanilla, or the occasional vanilla checkerboard. Even though I hadn't yet started the first grade, I fully embraced this life lesson. I intuitively recognized that ice cream was a metaphor for expansiveness, and that there was more to life than the familiar and the expected. Through this small act of kindness, Auntie Theresa taught me a monumental lesson, namely: you don't always have to go with what is ordinary. You could taste the nuances within the variety of life. You could always go with pistachio.

This photograph of Auntie Theresa was taken during the summer of 2016, at my dad's 80th birthday party.

The following summer, I saw Auntie Theresa again, at my sister's wedding. While she was very frail and confined to a wheelchair, she was still very much herself, and she was filled with love. At the end of the reception, when it was time to leave, I went over to say goodbye. I crouched down beside her wheelchair. Even though I was over 50 and we were in a large restaurant ballroom, my aunt held me like I was a baby, and she gave me unconditional love. I will never forget this.

Auntie Theresa passed away the following spring. She was 89 years old. Later that year, my cousins kindly included Dad when the family went out to celebrate what would have been Auntie Theresa's 90th birthday. When the check came, Dad tried to pay for his meal, and of course, my cousins wouldn't let him. Dad told Ginnie that Rob should not be allowed to pick up the tab, and Ginnie reassured him that this was coming from Auntie Theresa. It was so clear that, while she couldn't be there in person, Auntie Theresa was still very much present in spirit, and she was doing what she had always been doing. She was creating a feast for her family, just as she was creating continuity between worlds.

From Windowsills to Waterwheels

One of my favorite childhood memories of Dad took place on Valentine's Day, 1973. I was six years old, and in less than a week, Camille would turn five. My father was a school teacher, and my sister and I had to wait until mid-afternoon for his big white Chevrolet Impala to pull up the long driveway, so that we could run our special errand. We got into Dad's car and drove to Loft's Countryside Candies, a specialty candy shop in the next town over. While the shop was located on the side of a highway turnpike – and thus, nowhere near any body of water – the store nonetheless featured a waterwheel turning imaginatively on the side of the building. As a child, I thought this was fascinating, and I still remember staring at the waterwheel for a few minutes before entering the shop.

Once inside, it was like entering another world. I remember looking up and down the rows of sparkling glass cases, with light bouncing off all the shining surfaces. Behind the small windows were trays heaped with all types of dark and light chocolates. The aroma was sweet, rich, and heavenly. The best part of all was when Dad asked the clerk for not one, but three heart-shaped boxes. She handed him two small red cardboard boxes, and one much larger box for my mother. Dad walked over to a counter in the middle of the store and had the large box filled with "turtles," candies formed from chocolate-covered clusters of nuts and marshmallows. The miniature candy boxes held exactly four chocolates each, and Dad said that Camille and I could choose any candies we wanted. This was my first experience "chocolate shopping," and I felt very happy, knowing that these candies were a gift from my dad.

I love this story for so many reasons. First, there is the connection with my father. Once again, this story provides a window into a world that no longer exists, a place which, as Dad would say, "is a thing of the past." The waterwheel also taught me how to look at the familiar world in a different light. Just as the waterwheel served no practical purpose whatsoever, this decorative element turned something into something else – and in so doing, it was transformational.

Like so many of the stories that fill this book, in this narrative, knowledge of the world and knowledge of the heart are melded together. Looking at this childhood experience now, I can see that there is no reason not to see the heart-shaped box as another expression of Dad's heart, or of my own. Telling such stories creates a deeper and more cohesive sense of presence – and this too is a blessing, and a powerful piece of magic. Such energies keep things moving, much like the waterwheel that turns on the side of a building; a place that would only otherwise appear as an ordinary candy store by the side of the road, where there is no water.

V

THE DONKEY AND THE CUCUMBER: HOW WE LEARNED TO CURSE FROM THE MASTERS

Wipe the Floor With It!

In the tailor shop in Calabria, where my grandfather learned the trade, the Master Tailor was known for having a bad temper. As an apprentice in the shop, Grandpa not only learned how to be a tailor but, as Dad observed, he also "learned to swear from the Master Tailor in Italy. When your grandfather got mad, he would swear in Italian. He learned these curses from the Master."

One day, the tailor designed a custom wedding gown for a woman who was also known for having a difficult personality. As she went in for her fittings, the woman kept telling the tailor, "Adjust, adjust, adjust…" Finally, the tailor lost his patience. After the woman left the shop, the Master told Grandpa and the other apprentices, "Take that gown and wipe the floor with it!" So they did; they had to do what the Master told them. The boys dragged the white wedding gown all over the dirty floor, and then they hung it back up, and the tailor fixed it up a little. When the woman returned to pick up the gown, she said, "Beautiful!" Evidently, she never suspected that anything was wrong.

Hearing the story, I was horrified, and I wanted to make sure I was understanding everything correctly. So, I repeated the plot back to my father. "Oh yeah," Dad assured me, using a hybrid form of English and Italian, "This story comes from Mary Falvo, and you know Mary. She didn't exaggerate. No *che volare* the bullshit." In other words, Mary told the truth, and she didn't let anything fly.

Like many of the curses that were hurled in this world, "Wipe the Floor With It!" is a story of inversion, of flipping things on their head because they are seemingly too low or too high. While the wedding gown belonged to a woman who, the tailor felt, overstepped her boundaries and didn't show sufficient respect, telling the apprentices to drag the white gown all over the dirty floor represented a form of retribution – the payback of a curse. While the people in the shop all knew what happened, apparently, the woman never even noticed. Asymmetry of information is often key to the curses.

Dad also told me that, when he was little, Nannie left him at the tailor shop for a day. This was before Dad started school, and Nannie had to go to a funeral. A woman came into the tailor shop to have a garment altered. Grandpa marked the garment with tailor's chalk and, even as he did this, the woman kept wanting changes made. This frustrated Grandpa, and he said to her, "Lady, you are the limits out of the limits." This expression still makes Dad laugh. I asked if this was *all* that Grandpa said, or if he didn't add a little something extra, in Italian. Dad insisted no, not that time, but I still wonder about this. After all, back in Italy, he learned to curse from the Master.

The Wedding in Worcester: The Frames Were Too Tight

When it was time for Nannie and Grandpa to get married, Nannie's wedding gown came from Raphael's Department Store in downtown New Britain. While the story of their wedding is a blessing, there is another wedding-themed story concerning Nannie and Grandpa that is not exactly a curse, yet which describes a potentially serious mistake that caused considerable difficulty for one person, and only mild inconvenience for the other. As Dad tells it:

My father and mother got invited to a wedding
In Worcester, Massachusetts.
This was when Pa still owned the package store.
The wedding was on a Saturday,
And they couldn't both go.
One of them had to stay and run the store.
Because it was Pa who really knew these people,

They decided that he should be the one to go.
The wedding was all the way in Worcester –
So, a good distance away.
Pa took a whole carload of people
Up to Massachusetts with him.

When he left in the morning,
He put on my mother's eyeglasses, by mistake.
He didn't even realize what he had done,
And he was gone the whole day.
All that day, your poor grandmother
Had to struggle to see.
She had a really hard time,
But Pa didn't even notice.
He went all day long,
And he drove the car to and from Worcester.

When he got back later that night,
My mother told him that he took her glasses.
All he said was, "Oh, I felt that the frames
Were too tight.
I was going to bend them a little."
So while my mother struggled all day long,
Pa was only going to bend the arms of the glasses
A little bit,
Because the frames were too tight.

Ghostus!

In my family, there is one other story of a cursed wedding gown. Aunt Lucy was Nannie's younger sister, and one of three siblings who lived in the family home where Nannie grew up. The house was also the lifetime residence of Uncle John, Aunt Millie, and her husband, Uncle Bing. Uncle Bing was Greek, and Dad still remembers how, when he was a little boy, he saw Uncle Bing picking grape leaves from a vine in the back yard. At first, Dad thought Uncle Bing was crazy for picking the leaves rather than the fruit, but the next day, Dad ate stuffed grape leaves for the first time, and he loved them. As a child, this taught my father to keep an open mind about things.

Aunt Lucy never married, and everyone adored her. She always made you feel like you were the most important person in the world. Aunt Lucy would make wedding cakes, and on one occasion, she took care of a woman's wedding dress. Dad refers to this story as: "Ghostus!"

One time, somebody in the family was getting married,
And they got a wedding gown.
Your Aunt Lou was always so good about these things,
And she said she would take it and press it.
So she did – she pressed it,
And the only place she could see
To hang the long gown without wrinkling it
Was from a fixture in the living room.
So, she hung it there.

At that time, she lived downstairs,
And Aunt Millie and Uncle Bing lived upstairs.
Later that day everyone was out in the yard,
And they needed something from inside the house.
Uncle Bing went in to get it,
And he came running out again,
Calling "Ghostus! Ghostus!"

Uncle Bing was Greek, and he was a timid person.
As your Auntie Theresa would say,
He was afraid of his own shadow.
So, Uncle Bing thought there was a ghost in the house,
But it was just the wedding gown.

Apparently, the unexpected sight of a long white gown hovering in the living room frightened poor Uncle Bing. The wedding gown must have seemed otherworldly, like a spectral apparition that arose from a basic misunderstanding of the world. After Dad told the story, I said it was a good thing he didn't have a heart attack. Dad quickly replied, "He did. That's what killed him. He had a heart attack, but not from this. He had a hard job, buffing and polishing chrome appliances. He was a slight and timid person, and one day he did pass away from a heart attack."

Before Uncle Bing passed away, he had been planning to buy a new suit, but he didn't get around to it. After he died, Grandpa was asked to perform this task. He chose a suit for his brother-in-law, and he told the tailor how he wanted it altered. The tailor said to Grandpa, "We'd prefer for you to bring the person in," but Grandpa only said that he couldn't – he didn't tell them why. All the necessary adjustments were made, just as Grandpa had specified, and Uncle Bing was buried in that suit.

Like Close Cousins Who Live Across Town

There is far too much to say about Italian curses and blessings. Many Italian swear words are extremely well known in our culture, yet there is so much more to this fascinating subject than most people realize. While writing this book, I have come to appreciate the many ways in which curses and blessings often appear like intimate companions. They are closer than you think – a bit like first cousins who live across town, and who visit one another on the weekends.

In one sense, curses and blessings are categorical opposites. The orientation of a curse is typically negative, and the intention is to do harm, or take away another person's sense of power or well-being. In turn, blessings reinforce a positive sense of goodness, kindness, love, joy, peace, comfort, and compassion. While all of this is clear *prima facie*, when approached philosophically, things become more complicated. Curses and blessings often appear like opposites that attract; they reinforce and contrast with one another. Profanities are essentially profane. As such, they are intrinsically related to everyday life *and* to its opposite – to the sacred. Curses can seem either worldly or otherworldly, and sometimes they convey an imaginative perspective as ordinary life takes on a symbolic life all its own. Much like the Master Tailor's command to "Wipe the Floor With It!" or Aunt Mary from Hartford's unforgettable pronouncement that my cousin "should put it on the windowsill and slam the window down hard," many curses involve strategic acts of reversal. Such inversions express a corresponding sense of turning the world on its head, while thwarting someone or overturning an expectation that actually represents another way of flipping someone off. Some vulgar expressions are extremely imaginative, and a handful of curses are sheer marvels of creative invention. The more deeply you explore the issue of 'what is a blessing, and what is a curse?' the more you come to realize that this is really a hell of a good question.

As a child, I was exposed to a wide spectrum of unforgettable imagery. Sometimes, the curses centered on themes of revenge, sometimes they concerned people's inappropriate behavior, and occasionally, people's inept attempts to indulge in a cover-up. Sometimes, the curses were rooted in a basic misunderstanding of how the world actually works. Many of the curses emphasized a lack of proportion, and a corresponding sense of being out of balance with life. It was a bit like all that excessive housecleaning, except that the curses related to something dirty. Almost all of the phrases contained a sensual component, and they related to various states of human and animal embodiment.

If there is a pattern to the curses, it lies in the way the imagery relates to knowing the world through the flesh. These themes applied to issues of food and eating, marriage and sex. Some of the curses related to themes of family life, and they could be used ambivalently, either to reinforce a shared cultural ideal, or to express the ways in which these values became unbalanced or violated. The scope of these destructive creations is really quite impressive.

Finally, there are some curses that don't make sense until you hear the accompanying story, and even then – after the stories are carefully recounted and unpacked – the curses *still* don't fully make sense. Yet somehow, you just can't forget them. The next story is one of these.

Catch-a Benny!

"Catch-a Benny!" was a phrase I heard fairly often in childhood. Yet, when it was mentioned to me recently, I realized I had no idea what it *actually* meant. Perhaps this expression didn't mean anything at all? Did somebody just make it up? I had to know, so I got the story from Dad. He told me that Auntie Theresa and Benny went to high school together, and that Benny was very funny and always laughing. Benny's family lived in a residential section of town. One summer, Benny decided to construct a kind of portable shower out in the yard. Dad described it as the type of thing you would use to wash off, when getting into or out of a swimming pool. The shower was outside the house, and Dad said that Benny's "homemade creation must have been a mess. Benny's father was probably mad about this because he decided to pull the shower apart."

While Benny's father was outside dismantling the plumbing, he threw parts of the shower at Benny. Just as this was unfolding, a neighbor walked by and saw an older man throwing heavy metal objects at his teenage son. The father saw that the neighbor saw this, so he called out, in a loud voice with a thick Italian accent, "Catch-a-Benny!" This bit of quick thinking made it look as though this were some type of game they were playing, as though the older man was throwing shower parts *to* his son, not hurling plumbing *at* his son. Of course, everyone knew what was really going on.

It's easy to see how such a phrase becomes repeated over the years. It's just too good to forget. There is a perverse intelligence in all of this, a capacity for quick thinking when you've suddenly been caught in a bad situation, and you want to cover it up to avoid further embarrassment. Just as a person is discovered doing something they shouldn't be doing, they turn the situation on its head to make it appear like they are collaborating with – perhaps even, assisting – another person. It's intriguingly malicious because, when viewed through this lens, it looks like the recipient is somehow at fault if, for some reason, they don't anticipate what is coming and they fail to make the catch. So, a "Catch-a-Benny!" isn't just about projectiles; it is about deflection and deception. It is about the ability to think on your feet while you are hurling heavy objects at your own flesh and blood. It's a twisted example of how a good offense is sometimes the best defense (and sometimes not), and what a profoundly misguided version of this philosophy looks like in action. It looks a lot like hardware being flung across a suburban lawn on an otherwise quiet summer afternoon in Connecticut, as a neighbor casually strolls by.

I Don't Need That *Cataplasma*!

A few months after my mother passed away, Dad turned 80. After 50 years of married life, my father was now living independently. Just when I thought he could no longer surprise me, he managed to find a way. During one of our morning conversations, Dad told me that he was going to the YMCA to exercise, and that he would be seeing a friend there. Innocently, I thought, "Oh good… Dad has an exercise buddy." Of course, the story goes downhill from there.

This friend from the Y had asked Dad, now that his wife was gone, would he ever remarry or get a girlfriend? With a strong emphasis in his voice, Dad said, "No, I don't need that *cataplasma*!" Good God, I thought to myself, what is a *cataplasma*, and why does my 80-year-old father no longer feel the need for one? Dad was always so conservative. Could this be a euphemism for some kind of sex thing that people did back in the swinging 1960s, when he was last dating? Obviously, this was not something I wanted to contemplate further. We'll just gently move on, I thought to myself, and I'll smoothly change the subject. I'll ask Dad about his balance class at the Y… but before I could do this, the next words out of Dad's mouth were, "Aunt Millie always used to talk about that." At this point, all I could think is, "Worse and worse. If this has to do with Aunt Millie, this is not good, and it's not heading anywhere good."

Before continuing, let me provide a bit of context. I am a modernist art historian, and part of my academic training involves the study of European languages. Yet, for the life of me, at that moment, I could not figure out what a *cataplasma* was. Next, Aunt Millie was a rough diamond who did not mince words and who always spoke her mind. When Camille and I were little, she often served as our babysitter. Aunt Millie was always extremely good to us, far more than we deserved. Even though I knew we could be difficult little kids, she always called us her little *trina caro*, her little sweethearts (literally, her little lace hearts). Yet, when she was not babysitting us or talking with Nannie, Aunt Millie generally lacked a filter, and she was never one to shy away from discussing inappropriate subjects. Once Aunt Millie had to remind her sisters, "You know, I have a sense of humor!" Dad thought this was really funny, because everyone knew that Aunt Millie was usually so rough-edged and grouchy. All of which brings us back to the *cataplasma*.

Even with all my years of academic training, during that phone call, I could not figure out what a *cataplasma* was. Given that the term was being credited to Aunt Millie, I assumed it was something so awful that our parents had kept it from us as children, or perhaps, it could be something that Aunt Millie had simply made up. And, because Aunt Millie repeated this expression so often, it magically took on a life of its own, like "Catch-a-Benny!" While these possibilities flashed through my mind, Dad quickly picked up on my confusion, and he was already on the case. As though speaking to a small child who is not that intelligent, he patiently explained, "You know, a plaster cast."

This clue started me searching through the language databases in my mind, looking for terms relating either to sculpture or to medicine, including "plaster" and "cast." Plaster is *gesso* – this I know for certain. Could she be thinking of *calco*, for cast? Or, could she be thinking of plasma, like you would receive in a blood transfusion? Could this be a regional dialect kind of thing, or perhaps some odd pronunciation or inflection, because plasma sounds more like plaster than *gesso* does? What was she thinking? This began to take on the proportions of a research problem, so I became determined to figure this out. Consulting *The Bantam New College Italian & English Dictionary*, I saw that, while the medical term for plaster cast is *ingessaturà*, a *cataplasma* actually exists! Technically, the word refers to a poultice or plaster, but pejoratively, it means someone or something that is a bore.[10] Aunt Millie

---

[10] For the definitions of *cataplasma* and *ingessaturà*, see Melzi, *The Bantam New College Italian & English Dictionary*, pp. 94, 236.

was actually right about this. This took me about half an hour, but now we had a clear answer. Sort of.

My father still has good mobility, so the question remained as to why he did not need a plaster cast, or a *cataplasma*, particularly given that he didn't have a broken leg or a smashed finger (thank goodness). In Aunt Millie's metaphorical world, a *cataplasma* meant a burden, a load to carry, a heavy thing you didn't need and didn't want. These encumbrances could refer to anything from extra tax forms to fill out, to a heavy winter coat you had to lug around all afternoon. And yes, this term could refer to someone's spouse or partner. It was all coming back to me... Let's say that a woman was going out with a man the family did not approve of. This sentiment could cryptically be expressed as, "Hey, look at that one, over there! What's she doing with that *cataplasma*?" Then louder, across the room: "Hey Marie, how's the *cataplasma*?" Everybody would laugh out loud, and no one would have any idea what they were talking about. No one except each other, and that was just the way they liked it. As a burden to carry, a *cataplasma* is definitely a curse. So all I can say is, thank goodness my elderly father doesn't feel the need for one now.

They Made It Stink!

Just as a *cataplasma* is a metaphor for a weight that hangs heavily on the body, many of the curses express states of being that are known or experienced through the flesh. Virtually any organ or body part could be enlisted as a pathway for such cursed knowledge. The curses could encompass all five senses, including the nose and the sense of smell. Just as Nannie's world was all about balance and cleanliness, order and proportion, when something was excessive, my relatives would say with pronounced disgust: "They made it *stink*!"

This compact little phrase covers a surprising amount of ground. If someone made a toast at a party and they seemingly spoke for too long – and especially if the speech interfered with the vital activities of eating, drinking, or talking – then the person's perceived loquaciousness was dismissed as: "They made it stink! They didn't know enough to stop!" I'll never forget the gem of a time this expression surfaced at a reception following a funeral. The deceased person's niece spoke for what one of my relatives felt was far too long a time. Never mind that the poor woman had just lost her beloved uncle, and that she was deeply grieving. The food had been served, and it was already getting cold. The woman's tribute was taken as a decided imposition, so the judgment was, "She made it stink! She went on for too long!"

This unfortunate expression is not only offensive; it can be a game-changer. The phrase provides an efficient means for reframing a personal inconvenience so that the perceived offense is posed in collective terms. Thus, an individual annoyance or irritation becomes presented as a visceral response to excess, a kind of violation that ruins it for everyone else. It's as though a person is taking up far too much air, and their excessive behavior emits a distasteful odor throughout the entire room. After all, "They made it stink!"

'Bout-a-Time!

As a complement to "They made it stink!" we have what is known as a "'bout-a time!" At Saint Joseph's Church, the Sacrament of Confession was conducted during the afternoons. People would enter a darkened confessional booth where they would kneel down and confess their sins to a priest, who would be sitting on the other side of an opaque screen. The priest would hear the confession – say a blessing to absolve the person of their sins – and then assign a penance, which typically involved saying additional prayers. On the subject of confession, Dad related a story that kept us laughing for years: "'Bout-a-Time!"

Nannie and I were at church,
Waiting for our confession to be heard.
It was Easter time, and this happened on Holy Thursday.
We were sitting in the pews, waiting in line.
There was an older gentleman behind us.
He and my mother knew each other, so we said hello.
This man was related to
One of your grandmother's goomads.
The man's wife was having memory problems,
But he kept her at home.
He used to take her by the hand
And walk her all over the place.
He was a good person to do that.

So we're all sitting there in the pews,
And we're waiting, and waiting, and waiting.
When a younger woman finally came out
Of the confessional,
The man behind us blurted out, in a loud tone,
"It's a-bout-a-time!"
The woman kept walking toward the altar.
Nannie didn't say anything,
But she and I laughed.
After all, we did wait a long time…

Given that the elderly man was about to go to confession anyway, perhaps he didn't mind adding another item to the list? Whatever the case, the next time someone keeps you waiting because they take far too long to do something that should be simple, when they finally finish, you can think to yourself, "'bout-a-time!"

A Jackass of a Cucumber

In case you've ever heard the phrase "a *che ass* of a *jadrool*" and wondered just what it meant, the term denotes "a person who is a jackass of a cucumber." While, technically, the word for jackass is *asino* and cucumber is *cetriolo*, this is a stylized pronunciation that mixes Italian nouns with English articles and prepositions. It is another curse that doesn't fully make sense, even in translation. As a child, I would often hear this phrase, and I knew it was a rude way of saying that someone was unintelligent, or as Dad would say, "It's someone who is not too swift." By calling someone a *che ass* of a *jadrool*, you were able to reinforce your own sense of superiority through a dehumanizing expression that portrayed someone else as both obnoxious and slow. As I recall, this expression was a particular favorite when people were driving on the highway in heavy traffic.

Apparently, in Italian, if you call somebody a cucumber, this is like the English equivalent of saying that a person has the I.Q. of a houseplant. The image of the jackass speaks for itself, as this braying animal is known for being both stubborn and offensive. Yet this is colloquial Italian-American, so the composite curse takes on a life all its own. What emerges is a human-animal-vegetable combination; all that is missing is a mineral to make this particular insult a microcosm of the universe. Both the donkey and the cucumber are transformational.

The Evil Eye

Calling someone a *che ass* of a *jadrool* is a symbolic way of turning a human being into both a plant and an animal. Other curses engage the strategic usage of body parts in ways that are at once natural and supernatural. One of the most intriguing and disturbing of these is *malòc-chio*, the evil eye. Notably, this imagery evokes both an eye and a horn. *Malòc* relates to the word for bad (*mal*), while *occhio* is especially interesting because the term relates to both an eye *and a hook*. Thus if you were giving someone the evil eye or "the sign of *malòc*," you were essentially hurling a curse at a target, aiming the thought through your mind and your gaze, in order to hook or catch someone and have the ill-intention stick to them.

Wishing someone such intense harm was a serious curse, and it had its corresponding countermeasures. When Dad was growing up, if someone had a headache or didn't feel well, people would say that someone had given this person the *malòc*, and prayers would be said so that they "would pass the *malòc*." Grandpa's youngest sister, Aunt Mary Costanza, believed strongly in such forces. She would pray, and if she began to yawn, this was taken as a sign that the *malòc* would pass and the person would feel better soon.

The symbol of *malòc-chio* is fascinating because it is inherently ambivalent; it is an embodiment of both dark and white magic. *Malòc-chio* is associated both with a curse and with the blessing of protection from such curses and other forms of bad luck. It is the principle of repulsion through identification – using like to deflect like. The amulet for *malòc-chio* appears like a little curved horn. It is usually red or gold, and it is often worn on a chain around the neck, like a charm. This ambivalent symbol can thus represent both the evil eye and the lucky horn. Much like an animal horn, the token can be used either for offense or defense. As a protective force, medals with the sign of *malòc* were hooked on our diaper pins when my sister and I were infants; Camille recalls that Nannie and Mom used to have lively arguments over this.

Just as there are many ways of approaching the concept of *malòc*, Auntie Palma's husband, Uncle Leonard, took an alternative tack. Uncle Leonard was not of Italian heritage. As my cousin Gene reminded me, his father was an avid gun collector. When Auntie Palma and Uncle Leonard were first married, they lived in the same house with Aunt Millie.

One day, Aunt Millie was saying something about being afraid of the *malòc*, the evil eye. Hearing this, Uncle Leonard took a handgun out of his pocket, put it on the table, and succinctly said, "This will take care of the *malòc*."

Gouge in *Culo*

Making our way down the body, the rear end was always a favorite site for jokes and curses. Even Auntie Theresa, who was so patient and wonderful, would occasionally threaten to give someone a gouge in *culo* – a kick in the behind. Of course, we always knew this was an idle threat. The phrase was usually expressed as a kind of hypothetical possibility, as in, "You know what you'll get if you don't behave…" We never had to guess. We could have completed the sentence in our sleep, because the answer was always the same: "*a gouge in culo.*"

Speaking of ends, the end of a loaf of bread is called a *culaccino*, but the word became transformed depending on how it was used. The hard "c" was pronounced like a hard "g," so the end of a loaf of bread was commonly referred to as something that sounded like "goog-a-loon." In everyday usage, the phrase could be shortened even further, so that a person's rear end could be referred to as their "goog." While an overweight person would be described as having a large goog, for much of my life I have been on the thin side. As a teenager, I could easily squeeze between tight spaces in an overcrowded room, so I was affectionately known as "Goomada Skinny." Again, such embodied metaphors expressed cultural perceptions concerning balance and proportion. While Goomada Skinny is an Italian-English hybrid that refers to a woman who is seemingly too thin, her counterpart is a sexy woman with a large bottom.

My godfather, Goomba Tony, used to tell the story of how, in the 1950s, he heard a group of young men standing on a street corner, longingly referring to a woman with a shapely figure as "*Goomada Culo Turno.*" Translation: The boys were dreaming of their Godmother with the Invitingly Round Rear End. Even if this woman did not happen to be Italian, if she heard this phrase, she could take a pretty good guess at what they were saying, and she could start walking down another street.

He Saw More Ass than a Toilet Seat

The stories of ends don't end there. We're only just beginning, although I'll only share one more. Another unforgettable expression was associated with one of my distantly-related bachelor cousins. I only met this man once, when he knocked on our door one Christmas morning. Even though I was only a child, I immediately recognized that this man was a sharp dresser. What I could not have known was that he was a womanizer. As one uncle put it, "He had a reputation with the ladies." Or, as another uncle put it, "Oh yeah – he saw more ass than a toilet seat." This was yet another expression I was not supposed to have heard, which only made it funnier because it was stated on Christmas day.

Later that afternoon, when people were mentioning that this man had dropped by for a holiday visit, my uncles knew right away who this unaccustomed visitor was, and they identified him in the terms stated above. Once again, this was all about forms of forbidden embodied knowledge, so my uncles engaged a particularly vivid metaphor for expressing something "filthy," in the dual sense of being pornographic and scatological. Depending on who was using the phrase, it could either be a curse or a blessing, an expression of total disgust or of vicarious admiration. Either way, one thing was crystal clear: this man was having sexual relations outside the boundaries of marriage.

It goes without saying that no one would ever use such a phrase in front of Nannie, and she was certainly not pleased with this man's behavior. Dad recalls that, when he was a young man, Nannie strongly admonished him, "Don't be like your cousin! You get married!" Dad said that, at the time, this man was already on his way to being a bachelor, and that he stayed a bachelor all his life. Whether this was a curse or a blessing depended on your point of view. Either way, the vivid phrase exemplified people's perceptions of what were considered normative expressions of eros, marriage, and the family – and thus, matters of life and death themselves.

One Hundred Years!

At parties, a traditional Italian toast is *Chindon!* which means, "May you live for a hundred years!" This phrase is especially popular at birthday and anniversary parties, because it expresses a wish for a long life, or for a long life together. Either way, the words convey a blessing.

My father remembers Grandpa telling a story that put an unexpected twist on the phrase. At one of the clubs my grandfather belonged to, a birthday party was held for an extremely elderly man. During the party, the traditional toast was given: "*Chindon!* May you live to be 100!" Instead of being pleased, the elderly man became really angry. Apparently, no one knew his real age, so he told them, "I'm 99 – all of you want me to die?" In fact, the man did die before the year was over.

The inherent ambivalence of this story is fascinating. As with so many things, so much depends on your point of view, and of knowing how meanings operate within a given context. Flipping the themes of birth and death, this story describes the inversion of a celebration, just as it tells how a blessing inadvertently became a curse.

I Thought You'd Never Ask!

One of my grandparents' friends had a drinking problem. According to Dad, "He was a nice guy, and he was funny. He'd walk around with a shot glass in his pocket, and when he visited people, he'd pull the shot glass out and set it down on the table. Then he'd look at the person and say, 'Gee, I'd love one. I thought you'd never ask!'" While this story engages a certain type of inverted humor, it's also very sad. As with so many things, this is about excess and a lack of balance; in this case, using the lightness of hospitality and the charm of humor to cloak the darkness of a serious situation. Once again, everyone knew the truth of the matter.

Goodbye, I Go!

Another of my grandparents' friends liked to make homemade wine. This family consisted of a middle-aged couple and the man's elderly parents, who lived with them. At one point the family bought a new house, so they all had to move. The house they were leaving had many steps, and while transporting the heavy wine barrels, the older man fell down the stairs. As he fell, he called out to his son, "Goodbye, I Go!" Unfazed, the younger man turned around and said to his father, "Where the hell are you going? Get up!" The older man got up, and fortunately, he wasn't hurt. So, a "Goodbye, I Go!" is shorthand for a faux fatality, for someone thinking a situation is worse than it is, when it turns out to be not as bad as they had originally thought. It's a phrase of resilience; it is about the ability to see a blessing in what could have been a curse. This phrase represents another inversion, of knowing that this is not the end of the world, and that it is possible to get up again, even if you've dropped a heavy wine barrel down a steep flight of steps, and you've just gone down with it.

Testing the Brakes

Sometimes stories of "near misses" arise by accident, and sometimes they happen by design. In the latter case, they are often rooted in a fundamental misunderstanding of the world, in which a person acts without thinking things through. There are several of these stories in my family. The first one involves a misguided sense of judgment, because Dad's godfather, Goomba Pippie, wanted to make a larger statement about public safety. As Dad tells it:

My godfather was a good guy,
But he never drove a car.
Later in life, he worked as a school crossing guard.
He did the school crossings
On Farmington Avenue in Kensington,
And this was a busy street with a lot of traffic.
Day after day, he saw a certain car coming on pretty fast,
And there were a lot of people on this street.
So he thought to himself, "I'm going to test the brakes."

Goomba Pippie waited until the car came close,
And then he went right up to it
With his crossing guard paddle.
The guy slammed on his brakes and yelled out,
"Why did you do this?"
Goomba Pippie said, "I'm testing the brakes."

In my family, "Testing the Brakes" became shorthand for a well-intended but woefully misguided or reckless idea. This is all about playing with the edges, testing the limits of a situation, and clearly not thinking things through. Thank goodness this episode of "Testing the Brakes" did not turn out to be an actual "Goodbye, I go!"

You Hold It Tight, and I'll Go Get the String…

Another such story of misunderstanding how the world actually works involves genuine childhood innocence. One day, Nannie's brother and sister-in-law – Uncle Charlie and Aunt Bernie – went away and left their oldest daughter in charge. Dad said it was okay, even though the oldest girl had to work during the day, "The two other kids were old enough to be left alone during the daytime." The youngest was Dad's cousin, Donald, and he was somewhere between 10 and 12 at the time. On the day that Uncle Charlie and Aunt Bernie left, Donald went down to the cellar, and he saw that a water pipe had broken. Dad thinks it was actually the water main. Donald came back up the stairs and found his older sister, Elaine. Recognizing that there was a serious problem and wanting to address it, little Donald formulated a plan of action. He told his sister about the pipe, and he instructed her, "You go down there and hold it tight, and I'll go get the string to tie it." So the next time someone proposes a well-intentioned but totally inadequate response to a serious practical problem, you can think to yourself, "You hold it tight, and I'll go get the string…"

Wait a Minute—I've Got to Put My Glasses On

On the subject of people meaning well but not knowing what they are doing – with this lack of knowledge in no way stopping them – we have what is known as a "Wait a minute – I've got to put my glasses on."

One day, Grandpa's friend had a broken fingernail. Another friend said that he could fix it, so he reached into his back pocket and took out a jackknife. The man cut away at the nail for quite a while. Then he stopped and said to his friend, "Wait a minute – I've got to put my glasses on." This is a clear example of a person lacking clarity on what they should, and should not, be doing to another person. You may think you're doing somebody a favor, but you could be doing them a serious harm. In this case, the blessing of wanting to be a blessing was overshadowed by the curse of incompetence.

If He Liked You, It Was Another Story

Just as so many blessings and curses in this world are known through the flesh, my dad's first cousin, Mary Falvo, was a *cugina carne* – a blood relation, literally a cousin of the flesh. Mary was the daughter of Grandpa's sister, Francesca. Both Mary and her husband, Paul, were wonderful to my family. Like Grandpa, Paul was a tailor who learned the trade in Italy. While he was always extremely sweet and generous with us, Dad told me that Paul liked to curse at people. If Paul didn't like someone, he would call them *strunzo*. Dad always told me that this meant "someone who is not too swift," but of course, it is really a slang term for a piece of excrement. Beyond this simple epithet, one of Paul's favorite methods of cursing would be to wish unpleasant things on people he didn't like.

Mary and Paul had an extensive back yard, with wonderful gardens. Their next-door neighbor had a tall maple tree. The leaves would always blow into my cousins' yard, and Paul would have to rake them up. So, Paul wished a curse on the unsuspecting woman who lived next door: "I hope she grows taller than the tree!" Similarly, when the snowplow passed down the street and deposited snow in the apron of the driveway, which Paul then had to shovel out, he would see the snowplow coming and mutter, "I hope that guy chokes!" In retrospect, it seems that a lot of Paul's curses had to do not only with knowledge of the flesh, but with the practical aspects of home maintenance.

Don't All Small Children Get to Drink Black Coffee with Their *Fresenes*?

Personally, I have no memory of Paul's curses. When I told Dad how surprised I was to hear of Paul's swearing, especially because he was always so kind and generous with us, Dad chuckled and replied, "If he liked you, it was another story." The Falvos loved my father dearly, and they would give him all kinds of things to take home, especially produce from the garden, or homemade treats from Mary's kitchen. Mary's house was always immaculate, and she was an amazing cook. Dad told me that he didn't want to take so much, but Mary insisted. As she said to him, "If we have it, you have it. We're family."

One of the specialties I particularly associate with Mary is her *fresenes*. *Fresenes* are crunchy round biscuits flavored with anise seeds, and Mary's were heavenly. When we came to visit, Mary would serve fresh *fresenes* in the afternoon, along with fragrant, freshly percolated coffee. Even though I was only a child, I can remember sitting at her kitchen table having coffee and *fresenes* on a sunny afternoon. I always liked my coffee mild, mixed with a lot of milk, but my sister – who is almost two years younger than me – thought that the *fresenes* tasted better with black coffee. So, Mary allowed Camille to have this! All of which meant that, growing up, I thought all little kids were allowed to have black coffee with their afternoon *fresenes*, if they asked very nicely. No matter what age you were, Mary's coffee and *fresenes* could only be a blessing, as known through the flesh.

Fresenes

Ingredients

5 lbs. flour

10-12 eggs

¾ to 1 cup Crisco

1 ½ tablespoons sugar

1-2 tablespoons salt

2 tablespoons black anise seeds

A good-sized piece of yeast

Directions

Make like bread – when golden, take them out, split in half, round the edges to form circles, and re-bake on a cookie sheet.

The Infant of Prague

Like so many of my relatives, Mary was extremely religious. Yet unlike anyone else, Mary had a holy statue propped up against the pillows of her bed. To my child's eyes, this statue looked very much like an elaborate doll. When I asked my mother about this, she told me it was the Infant of Prague – a holy statue of the child Jesus, dressed in a ceremonial gown, wearing a crown and holding a globe. As a little girl, I had some difficulty understanding why my middle-aged cousin would have such a special doll on her bed, especially one that she didn't actually play with. As an adult, I recognize that Mary's Infant of Prague was a particular type of sacred presence, a holy figure that could be seamlessly integrated within the intimate spaces of a domestic setting. Perhaps the Infant of Prague was particularly needed in that house, to offer blessings to offset the curses that were uttered in the back yard if Paul didn't like you. But if he liked you, it was another story…

VI

THE ONGOING LIFE
OF THE LIVES:
THE BLESSINGS OF THE STATUES,
THE VISIONS, AND THE NEAR-
DEATH EXPERIENCES

The Stories of the Statues

While Mary Falvo's statue of the Infant of Prague was a bit unusual, devotional objects were familiar presences in homes like the one I grew up in. These holy objects could include freestanding sculptures, crucifixes, rosary beads, prayer cards, or holiday ornaments. Such a crucifix hung by the bedroom door of the room that my sister and I shared while we were growing up.

Crucifix with a Palm Sunday Cross

While these religious objects held clear spiritual meanings, many of these same items were associated with everyday concerns, as well. This was certainly the case with the statue of the Blessed Virgin that my mother put on the pantry windowsill when she wanted good weather. Just as these sacred figures were associated with the transcendent, so too were they deeply integrated within domestic settings, where they were actively used. As a result, these sacred presences became blended with the most familiar and mundane aspects of life itself. In houses like the one I grew up in, such sacred objects were *living presences* because they were actively a part of our lives. We lived with them, and they lived with (and within) us.

Statue of Saint Joseph Holding the Christ Child

From the earliest time I can remember, two holy statues stood on my father's dresser. One was a sculpture of the Carmelite nun Saint Thérèse of Lisieux, the Little Flower. One of Saint Thérèse's most powerful insights is that the sacred is often found in the most ordinary of places. The story of this sculpture appears at the end of this chapter.

Opposite Saint Thérèse was a statue of Saint Joseph, the father of Jesus. In this image, Saint Joseph is portrayed as a middle-aged man wearing flowing brown and cream-colored robes that are trimmed with green. In his arms, he holds the Christ Child and some Easter lilies. A dime was always placed in the crook of Saint Joseph's arm, right beside the flowers.

While Saint Joseph served as the patron saint of our home, this statue came from the Irish side of the family. After my parents were married, the sculpture was a gift from my mother's father, Grandfather Cosgrove. As Dad explained, "Your grandfather brought this statue to the house. In those days, you put a dime on it. The philosophy was that, if you kept the dime on it, you'd always have money for the house, which we did."

How I Started Working With Wood

Saint Joseph is the patron saint of fathers and families, of immigrants and carpenters. My father was an Industrial Arts teacher, and woodworking was his specialty. Our home was furnished with many beautiful pieces of furniture that he built himself. One morning, Dad told me the story of: "How I Started Working With Wood."

> When I was little, Sonny made a gig.
> It was a little car, with pulleys and ropes.
> It had a steering wheel that really worked.
> He was talented, to put this thing together.
> When he got tired of it, I took it over.

For the wood to make the hood of the car,
I'd go to the grocery store down on the corner,
And I'd get orange crates.
They were made of wood,
And they came in two sections.
I'd take the large crates apart,
Save the nails so I'd have nails to use,
And then I'd cut the wood
To make the pieces for the car.
I'd make the angles, and I didn't do a very good job.
I didn't get any training until the seventh grade.

When I was a kid, a mother and daughter were living
On the third floor of the house.
I didn't know it then,
But the highlight of their evenings
Was to watch me work outside.
I wasn't very old –
I was maybe, seven or eight at the time,
And that's how I started to work with wood.

It Sits In a Place of Honor

Later in life, Dad bought a second, smaller statue of Saint Joseph. This sculpture depicts Saint Joseph, not as an older man and a father, but as a young carpenter. The figure wears a work apron, and he holds a saw in his right hand and a tool chest in his left.

Statue of Saint Joseph as a Carpenter

Another of Saint Joseph's attributes is that he helps to sell property. My father bought the little statue when he was 70 years old and he wanted to sell the family homestead and move into a more efficient townhouse. Dad would not buy the new property until he had sold the original house, so he acquired the little statue, and he told me the story of how: "It Sits In a Place of Honor."

> The Saint Joseph statue is only a little statue,
> But it sits in a place of honor
> On the mantelpiece over the fireplace.
> I was told that, to sell property,
> You are supposed to bury the statue of Saint Joseph
> Upside down, outside the house.
> But, I wouldn't hear of it!
> Your mother put the statue
> In the front porch of the old house,

But pointing in the direction of the new place.
Within five days of getting the statue,
The family home sold.
Three people saw the property,
And there were three offers within five days.

This story exemplifies the ways in which religious objects could be associated with everyday concerns. While my mother worked her windowsill magic – engaging the sacred for secular purposes – my father attended to the practical details of carpentry and real estate transactions, and everything turned out well.

My Aunt's Rosary Beads

After Auntie Florie passed away, I asked her son George if there was a small token that I could have to remember her by. The item could be extremely modest, but I wanted something that had belonged to Auntie Florie herself. A short time later, we were all together at a family wedding. George told me that they had not kept many mementos from the house, but they did have something for me. He handed me a small package, and he explained that this item was not valuable, but that it was very important to Auntie Florie. As I unwrapped the tissue paper, I saw a set of blue and white rosary beads. George told me that his mother was a good Christian. She used these rosary beads in rehab when she was elderly and frail, and she was holding them at the end of her life. As he said these words, and I held Auntie Florie's rosary beads in my own hands, I felt a thrill pass straight through me, and tears came to my eyes. My cousin was a bit surprised that I was so moved by this small gift. Yet there was a larger story in play, which he could not have known. But I knew, and I saw multiple pathways crossing before my eyes.

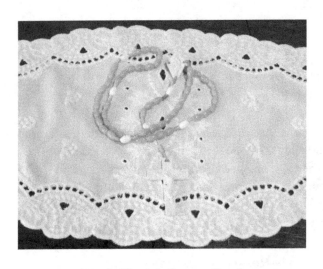

Auntie Florie's Rosary Beads

In addition to my work as a literary artist in Palliative Medicine at the M. D. Anderson Cancer Center, I work with a Rehabilitation Medicine population in the Mechatronics and Haptic Interfaces (MAHI) Lab at my university, Rice University. Spinal cord injury patients and amputees come to campus to participate in the experimental studies in upper extremity robotic therapies conducted there.

Much as in my work at M. D. Anderson, I visit with people, and we discuss themes that are significant and meaningful for them. As we talk, I record their words verbatim, and I arrange their phrases into successive lines that resemble poetry. I then read the narratives aloud while making any changes or corrections that they indicate. Finally, I inscribe the stories into a journal, which the person is able to keep as a gift.

As I do this delicate work with a Rehabilitation Medicine population, I carry Auntie Florie's rosary beads in a silk pouch in my tote bag, just as I carry Auntie Theresa's rosary beads when I work with terminal cancer patients at M. D.

Anderson. While rosary beads are associated with the traditional practices of Roman Catholicism, these same objects evoke the warmth of domestic spaces and the familiar presences of my beloved aunts. As multiple worlds come together, I can feel my aunts' presences with me, in spirit.

A Lady All Dressed In Blue

On both my mother's and my father's sides of the family, various people have had near-death experiences, end of life visions, and transcendent encounters. Just as the spiritual and the domestic, the sacred and the profane, are deeply interwoven within this world, so too do people's corresponding visionary states appear to be multiple. Among the close presences of family, friends, culture, and community, numinous and ordinary subjects walk hand in hand.

Grandpa passed away at home on December 7, 1961. Dad told me that, before he passed, Grandpa shared a vision of: "A Lady All Dressed In Blue."

Just before he died –
It was a few days before he passed –
Your grandfather had fallen asleep
In a reclining armchair.
When he woke up, he told your grandmother
That a lady came to him,
A lady all dressed in blue.
He thought it was the Blessed Virgin Mary.

Many years later, Pa's friend was dying.
The man looked toward the foot of the bed
And he said to his wife,
"Can't you see him?
My friend Camillo is there, and he came to see me.

Didn't you see him?"

So, Pa had come to see his friend.

Nannie passed away on December 18, 1992. While Dad never knew of Nannie having any end of life visions, Auntie Florie told my father that, the night before she died, Nannie attended a holiday program. The nun who had been present throughout, told my aunt that, the night before she passed, Nannie was so happy, singing with the group.

When Uncle Sonny was facing the end of his life, he told Auntie Theresa that he knew he was dying. While this knowledge reflected Uncle Sonny's intuitive sense of his own mortality, his insight nonetheless struck the family as uncanny. As Dad put it, "I don't know how he knew." Like all of the siblings, Uncle Sonny had a gift for entertaining, and he and Auntie Terry used to host wonderful family parties on both New Year's Day and the Fourth of July. At his last Fourth of July party, Uncle Sonny made homemade sausage. Knowing how much my father loved his homemade sausage, Uncle Sonny encouraged Dad to eat some. As he affectionately said, "Who else makes this for you?" A few days later, Uncle Sonny passed away.

While this story is very poignant, other family stories are at once metaphysical and extremely practical, sometimes to the point of being humorous. Like both my mother and my father, on several occasions, Auntie Theresa nearly passed away. During the 1930s, both she and Dad contracted diphtheria – a potentially deadly illness. She had to be confined to the house for extended periods of time while Nannie took care of her. Later in life, Auntie Theresa had to have heart valve replacement surgery, and she did not respond well to the standard cardiac protocol. In the days following the procedure, Auntie Theresa lay in a non-responsive state. When she woke up, she told several family members that, while she was asleep, she had been talking to Auntie Palma on the telephone. Auntie Palma had passed away a few years before, and as Auntie Theresa described their conversation, it was clear that she felt very close to her older sister.

Through a Thick Glass Window

When Dad was very young, he nearly died twice from two unrelated medical conditions. As a child, he scratched a mosquito bite on his leg, and it turned into Erysipelas. The infection entered a vein and traveled up his leg, heading toward his heart. The family doctor injected a new drug directly into Dad's vein; this was an experimental therapy that preceded penicillin. The procedure was very risky, but the gamble paid off. This intervention saved my father's life.

Within less than a year, Dad suffered a second life-threatening illness. When diphtheria struck, Auntie Theresa was confined to the house, but Dad was sent to an isolation hospital in Hartford. At this facility, my grandparents could only view him through a thick glass window. Dad was very young at the time, and he still remembers how he would cry and cry when his parents had to leave. After a while, Nannie and Grandpa saw that Dad was not getting any better. They decided to take him home, acting against the authority of the hospital. Once at home, the family doctor took care of him and he recovered. The visiting nurse also came to see him twice a day, once as part of her standard daily routine, and the second time, on her own initiative.

As a side note to this story, many years later Grandpa bought a new Plymouth. The car was parked on the road outside the house, and Grandpa was sitting in the sun parlor when he saw the car get hit. He went outside, and he immediately recognized the person who had hit his new car – it was the same visiting nurse who had cared for his son, so many years before. When Grandpa saw who it was, he had no concern about the car. Yet Dad was a teenager, and he did. He said to his father, "Can't you see that the car is all damaged?" Grandpa replied, "It doesn't matter. She saved your life. I told her to go home and not worry about it. If it weren't for her, you wouldn't be here." Grandpa took the Plymouth to an auto body shop, and he paid for all of the repairs himself. He was happy to do it. This woman had saved his son's life.

In Showroom Condition

A few months after my mother passed away, Dad developed acute congestive heart failure. It was the same year he turned 80, and he had to be hospitalized on Christmas day. After he came home, Dad shared a dream he had experienced. He and I had been talking about cars – one of Dad's favorite subjects – and it triggered his recollection:

> I had a dream I was with your grandfather,
> And he and I were looking at your grandfather's car.
> It was a 1936 Lafayette Sedan.
> That car was made the same year I was born,
> And it was beautiful,
> With a dark blue exterior and a tan interior.
> The Lafayette was made by the Nash Company,
> And they didn't make that many of them.
> So, I said to Pa,
> "This car has got to be worth a lot of money.
> It's in showroom condition."
> I remember this because
> I don't dream about the family that often.

Dad loves for everything to be neat and pristine, and above all, he loves for cars to be this way. For my father, the phrase "in showroom condition" represents the highest praise, and this dream made him very happy. Yet hearing him speak, I knew what I was hearing. Intuitively, I felt that we were all being put on notice, and I had several follow up questions. Our conversation went something like this:

"Okay, were you in the car driving somewhere, or just looking at it?"

"No, we were just looking at it."

"Was Nannie there, too?

"No, it was just me and Pa."

"Did Grandpa say anything to you?"

"No, it was just us and the car."

This story made me both sad and joyful. The car is a transitional image that appeared in the wake of Dad's near-death encounter with acute congestive heart failure. While my father is deeply religious and his faith is almost otherworldly, the image of the Lafayette Sedan is about as secular as you can get. Once again, the character of the dream is multiple, as a sense of visionary spirituality is closely associated with everyday objects and with the familiar presences of people who have passed on. The dream is a gift, but it is not an easy gift to accept. Both literally and metaphorically, the dream is a vehicle, a gift that allows us to visualize the transition and the journey. When the time comes, Grandpa and Dad will travel together in style, in a beautiful car that was made the same year Dad was born. The car will be in showroom condition, exactly the way my father likes it. He will be with his father, and everything will be new again.

The Bright Light All Around

I strongly believe that the near-death encounters that both of my parents experienced in childhood brought them closer together, as adults. These experiences undoubtedly shaped how they lived their lives. My parents engaged in various forms of service work. Before she was married, my mother was a school librarian; later in life, she volunteered as parish librarian for Saint Joseph's Church. When my sister and I went off to college, Mom spent 13 years working as a Home Health Aide. As an undergraduate, she had initially been drawn to the nursing profession, but then she switched to the field of Library Sciences. When the house was empty, Mom went back to work "to fulfill her dream of nursing." In this capacity, she went into the homes of the ill and the elderly, providing care to vulnerable people. In turn, my father spent his entire professional career in the public school system. He also did extensive volunteer work. For more than three decades, he served as a Minister of Communion in his parish church. He held the title of Extraordinary Minister of the Eucharist, and for many years, he brought the sacrament to convalescent homes and assisted living facilities, where he also conducted services. Throughout their lives, both of my parents were active in their communities, where they engaged in various forms of service in the fields of education, healthcare, and religion.

My mother's first near-death experience occurred when she was seven years old, in January of 1948. During the 1940s, women and girls commonly wore hats when they dressed up, and these hats were held in place by large hatpins. One Sunday morning, my mother had returned home from church. She took off her hat and placed the hatpin in her mouth. She then went to take off her coat, tilted her head backwards, and accidentally swallowed the pin. Mom had to undergo extensive abdominal surgery, and she was hospitalized for a month following the procedure. For the rest of her life, she bore a long scar that indicated the length of the incision. Undoubtedly, she lost a good deal of blood during the procedure, and she had a near-death experience on the operating table. Along with the physical presence of the scar, my mother carried this spiritual experience with her throughout her entire life: "The Bright Light All Around."

All I remember
Is that there was a lot of bright white light,
Not the kind that blinds you,
Just bright white light.
In the middle was Christ, the man.
He was a full-grown man,
And he looked like the man you see
In the pictures of Christ.

What I remember is,
I wanted to stay,
And I couldn't stay.
I tried to go forward,
And this large light blocked me.
He said I had to go back and help people.
I was just there, standing in front of him.
I was perfectly content looking at the light,
And looking at him,
And I had no desire to go anywhere.
But that's what he said,
And he sent me back.
Then everything faded,
And when I woke up,
I was in the recovery room.

I remember it very vividly.
I remember the bright light all around,
And being surrounded by bright light.
It didn't bother me to look at him,
Or to look at it all.
When I was looking at him,
I felt happy, and secure, and loved.

When I asked Mom if this experience changed her life, she said, "I suppose it did. It made me more considerate and thoughtful of other people. These experiences got me through difficult times and helped me later in life."

Dad Will Be Coming To Visit

Throughout her life, my mother struggled with poor health. During her final hospitalization, she was on the Acute Care Unit in respiratory failure, intubated and on a ventilator. While she could no longer speak, she used a whiteboard to communicate. She and her father, Grandpa Cosgrove, had been very close. One of the last things Mom expressed to my sister was: "Dad will be coming to visit." Knowing of my mother's proclivity for visionary spirituality, I immediately accepted this statement at face value and quickly asked my sister, "Yes, but did she say *when?*" Hearing this, Camille laughed out loud, and I laughed with her. I was so grateful that we could laugh together, in that moment of all moments.

Like Red Velvet

During my mother's funeral service, I shared another of her spiritual visions. One of Mom's loveliest qualities was her sense of generosity. She was one of those people who truly loved helping others. She would give you the shirt off her back, and then she'd go to the store to buy a second shirt, not for herself, but for you. Reading her words aloud, it felt like she was there with us, in spirit: "Like Red Velvet."

Many years ago they had a priest come
To give a mission at Saint Joseph's.
And at the very end,
He had the power to give a special blessing,
Which took away all the sins we ever committed
In our life up to that point,

And he gave it at the end of Mass.

I didn't leave right away,
Because I was flooded with an interior love so strong,
I felt it wrap around me,
And hold me so tightly,
And I could see the color red.
It was like a bolt of red cloth,
A deep red like red velvet.
It didn't last long, but the experience was,
I was so loved that,
If I had died right then,
I would have gone
Straight to heaven.

After sharing this story, my mother also told me about her sense of: "Inner Peace."

The other night I was settling down,
And I had this beautiful feeling of peace,
That everything was going to be alright,
You know, an inner peace.

It didn't last very long,
But I did have it for a while.
It happens every once in a while.
You can have permission to write this.
I don't mind sharing.

That was my mother. She didn't mind sharing.

Multiple Names, Multiple Lives, Multiple Worlds

My mother's full name is Joan Marcia Cosgrove Gagliardi. Her parents were Irish-American, and her maiden name reflects the heritage of her birth, just as her married name signifies my father's Italian-American family identity.

While growing up, Auntie Theresa was the aunt I was closest to. Her full name is Theresa Rose Gagliardi Glownia. Both her first and middle names indicate that she is named for Saint Thérèse of Lisieux, the Little Flower. Rather than using the saint's historical French name, my family always used the Italian variation, calling her Saint Theresa. Auntie Theresa's maiden name is the same as my father's, while her last name is her married name.

My full name is Marcia Theresa Gagliardi Brennan. My first name is my mother's middle name, my middle name resonates with both Saint Thérèse of Lisieux and Auntie Theresa, my maiden name is my Italian-American family name, and in marriage, I took my husband's last name, which reflects our shared Irish-American heritage. Thus all of our names are hybrids, and each tells a story.

My father always had a statue of Saint Thérèse of Lisieux on his dresser, opposite the figure of Saint Joseph. In this sculpture, Saint Thérèse is dressed in the black veil and white cape that comprise the traditional habit of the Carmelite nun. She looks ahead as she carries her cross in her arms, surrounded by a bouquet of red and white roses.

Statue of Saint Thérèse of Lisieux, the Little Flower

When we were children – and especially, when we were causing trouble – Dad would always say a short prayer that began "*Madonna Mia*," and which ended by asking Our Lady of Mount Carmel to help us all. This is a prayer to the Virgin Mary in her role as patroness of the Carmelite Order, of which Saint Thérèse was a member. The statue of Saint Thérèse was a gift to my father from Auntie Theresa. Several years later, a third statue appeared on Dad's dresser. This smaller, black and white ceramic statue of a nun with a golden cross and golden rosary beads was also a gift from Auntie Theresa.

Statue of a Nun Holding a Devotional Offering

Yet, well before the little black and white statue appeared, there was the colorful statue of Saint Thérèse, and this object has its own special story. When my mother told my father that they were going to have their first child, Dad truly wanted a little girl. As he told me, "I prayed to Saint Theresa that I would have a little girl, so your Auntie Theresa gave me this." This was during the mid-1960s. When I was being born, Dad sat in the Father's Waiting Room at the local hospital, saying novenas to Saint Thérèse, praying for a little girl. When I arrived, he named me for this saint.

I Just Had to Show You That Rose

Both Nannie and Auntie Theresa were a lot like Saint Thérèse – they loved their work, and they loved to sprinkle love on everything. They also loved roses. While we were growing up, red roses bloomed on the white arch that stood in the back yard, by the pantry window. Auntie Theresa also had a little flower garden planted along the wall by her back porch. One day, when we were visiting, a particularly vivid, coral-pink rose was just about to flower. I was a teenager at the time, and in my mind's eye, I can still see the rosebud on its long green stem, so lush and radiant on that warm summer afternoon. Just as we were walking toward the house, Auntie Theresa called me over to the back porch. Everything was done very quietly. My aunt leaned forward and said to me, "I just had to show you that rose."

This tender story pre-figures an extremely powerful end of life vision that occurred many decades later. On October 8, 2014, Auntie Theresa called to tell me about a vivid dream in which she was visited by Saint Thérèse. At that time, my aunt was grappling with the symptom burden associated with the treatment of multiple myeloma; she would pass away three and a half years later. As we spoke, she described how on some days she felt weak, with low energy levels and a spongy feeling in her legs. Yet as she related her vivid dream of Saint Thérèse, the conviction in her voice was unmistakable. Her tone was filled with strength and joy as she emphasized how taken she was with the saint's beautiful little smile, and with the short-stemmed red rose. As she told me:

It was Saint Thérèse's feast day on October first,
And Saint Thérèse came to me in a dream.
It was some time between midnight and dawn.
She was carrying her cross with her, with the red roses,
And she handed me a rose.

It was a short-stemmed red rose, with a tight bud.
She didn't take it from her cross.
She already had it in her right hand.
All she did was look at me,
And hand it to me.
I think it was designated for me.
She just handed it to me, so gently.

And I mean – it was real.
She was there.
It wasn't really a dream.
That's the truth.
I could feel her.
She was so serene, so peaceful,
And I knew to have faith, that I was going to be okay.
I was just filled with serenity.
It was the most beautiful thing.

I've been seeing roses all over, even today.
Saint Thérèse was so peaceful,
She just handed the rose to me so gently.
It was the most beautiful thing.
I can still see her handing me that rose.

Much as in my work at the M. D. Anderson Cancer Center, when speaking with my aunt, I recorded her words verbatim and arranged the phrases in successive lines that resembled poetry. After she had finished, I read the story back to her, and I invited her to make any additions or corrections that she wished. When my aunt heard her story read aloud, she almost couldn't believe the beauty of her own words, as her life experience became transformed into a poetic narrative.

She then expressed her gratitude, and she gave me permission to share the story.[11]

---

[11] This conversation marked the beginning of another book I am writing, which is entitled *A Rose From Two Gardens: Saint Thérèse of Lisieux and Images of the End of Life* (forthcoming from the University of California Medical Humanities Press). Drawing on my creative clinical practice as an Artist In Residence in Palliative Medicine at the M. D. Anderson Cancer Center, I trace the intriguing parallels that arise between contemporary end of life images and themes expressed historically in the writings of Thérèse of Lisieux (1873-97), the Catholic saint who is known as the "Little Flower". My aunt's imagery will provide the opening story, while the narratives that follow will be drawn from the clinical work. Notably, Auntie Theresa's story also represents an example of what the historian of religion Robert A. Orsi has characterized, in another context, as an intimate history in which "family dynamics are one spring of sacred presences". In such narratives, spirituality unfolds within "experience and practice, in relationships between heaven and earth, in the circumstances of people's lives and histories, and in the stories people tell about them". See Robert A. Orsi, *Between Heaven and Earth: The Religious Worlds People Make and the Scholars Who Study Them* (Princeton: Princeton University Press, 2005), pp. 13, 18.

Lyn Smallwood, *That Rose Was Designated For Me: Saint Thérèse of Lisieux*, 2015, pencil on white Arches paper

Shortly after our conversation, I asked the West Coast visual artist Lyn Smallwood to illustrate the narrative. *That Rose Was Designated For Me: Saint Thérèse of Lisieux* depicts the saint carrying her familiar attribute of a cross surrounded by a cluster of roses. The delicate lines of the fine pencil drawing form the sweeping folds of the traditional white cape and the dark veil that comprise the habit of the Carmelite nun, while Thérèse's facial features display her characteristically tender gaze and gentle smile. Much as in my aunt's dream, the saint appears to be standing in a three-quarter view as she turns to offer the viewer a single, short-stemmed rose.

While talking with my family, and while working in the hospital and in the lab, people's stories often take on poetic forms. As I noted in the Introduction, when love comes into the stories, the prose can read like poetry. In my own mind, I think of this as the poetry of the in-between. The flowing words show the subtle ways in which love can conjoin multiple worlds, particularly worlds that might otherwise appear to be separate. Just as I carry Auntie Florie's rosary beads with me when I work with Rehabilitation Medicine populations at Rice, I carry Auntie Theresa's rosary beads when I work with cancer patients at M. D. Anderson. Again and again, the connection is love, and there are all different types of love and levels of knowing.

Auntie Theresa's Rosary Beads

In all cases, writing about the ones who have passed and the ones who are here brings these worlds closer together. The stories that fill this book can teach us how to see the presence within the presence, *and* how to recognize the presence beyond the presence. In this way, the stories expand the scope of life itself. Even though many of the worlds I write about no longer exist, this book is both a cultural heritage document *and* a study in living presences. This is both mind-blowing and heart-opening. If I were to clothe this insight in a metaphorical image, I might say that it looks a lot like opening and closing a window.

EPILOGUE

THESE THINGS MEAN A LOT TO US:
THE STORY AFTER THE STORY

Just as this book was going to press, my Dad passed away. He lived independently in his own home until the last two weeks of his life. Before his final illness, I was able to share with him that the book had gone under contract with a publisher. Dad was very proud, and he loved the brief description that I read aloud to him over the phone. This was the only part of the book that he was able to hear. On the morning of Saturday, September 7, 2019, I stood at the lectern of Saint Joseph's Church and read my father's own words on how "You Only Have One Family, You Don't Have More" and "In Showroom Condition" to honor him at his funeral service. The journey had come full circle. I stood reading Dad's words at the same church where he had been baptized 83 years before.

After Dad passed, my sister had the task of clearing out the townhouse and identifying the items that were of value and which should be kept within the family. In the process, Camille found two of Dad's rings, one of which held the diamond that had originally belonged to Nannie's engagement ring. After Nannie passed away, Dad had the diamond reset in a ring for himself. The gold band of Nannie's engagement ring was gifted to me when I received my Master's degree from Brown University. I held onto this ring for more than 20 years, and I recently gave the ring back to my sister, so that the diamond could be restored to its original band and, one day, given to my niece. This idea resonated with my work in assembling the narratives for this book. In all cases, the larger plan was to reunite the original elements, and then, to pass them down. Camille told me that, when she found Dad's two rings, she also found

A piece of paper with Nannie's wedding ring taped to it.

It said: Nannie's wedding ring,

The date they were married, and

Give to Rob.

I dropped it off with Rob.

Just a nice story.

Our cousin was understandably moved by this tender gesture. These things mean a lot to Rob. They mean a lot to me, as well.

MORE RECIPES

Nannie Never Used a Recipe

When she cooked, my grandmother never used a recipe. She did everything by hand and by eye, informed by a lifetime's worth of knowledge. The only reason we have these recipes at all is because of my mother. When my Irish-American mother married my father in 1965, she wanted to make him happy. My mother was not a cook; she was a librarian, and she wrote everything down by hand. The recipes exist in written form because my mother recorded them on 3 x 5 inch index cards. All of the recipes that appear in this book are typed transcriptions of *all of the information* that was written on the index cards. Nothing has been left out, and this is literally all that we have. In one sense, my mother's recipe box can be viewed as a kind of cultural heritage archive. In another sense, the recipes provide a tangible means to recreate the sense of being with someone in spirit. Thus the recipes have multiple lives, including those that continue through such inter-generational channels of transmission.

While I spent many years watching Nannie and my aunts cook many beautiful dishes, I do not have the gift of cooking. To repeat: *I am not a cook. I am a writer. If you make any of these recipes yourself, please do not write to me with questions about how to prepare, cook, or serve the dishes. I will not know the answers, and any answer I would give would inevitably be wrong.* While the recipes are blessings, taking cooking advice from me would only be a curse – and thus, a recipe for disaster.

Cream of Carrot Soup

Ingredients

1 large onion, chopped

2 cloves of garlic, crushed

1 tablespoon olive oil

1 pound of carrots, chopped

1 teaspoon mixed herbs

1 ½ pints vegetable stock – 2 cans

¼ pint sour cream

Salt and pepper

Directions

Prep time 10 minutes; Cook time 35 minutes

Sauté the onion and garlic in oil until transparent.

Add carrots, mixed herbs, and stock.

Boil for about 30 minutes until carrots are soft.

Cool and then liquidize until smooth.

Add sour cream, season to taste, and mix thoroughly.

Heat through gently, making sure the soup does not boil, then serve.

Rich Brown Soup

Ingredients

2 ounces butter or margarine

2 ½ ounces flour

1 ¼ pints water

¾ pint beef stock

Salt and pepper

Dash of Worcestershire Sauce

Grated cheese

Fresh parsley for garnish

Directions

Prep time 30 minutes; Cook time 2 hours

Heat butter or margarine until melted. Sift in flour, then cook over low heat, stirring until flour is rich brown in color.

Gradually stir in water and stock. Stir constantly, to prevent lumps from forming.

Add salt, pepper, and Worcestershire Sauce. Cover and simmer slowly for 2 hours.

Serve sprinkled with grated cheese and garnish with parsley.

Eggplant Parmigiana

Directions

Slice eggplant. Put in a colander and sprinkle salt. Drain for 2 hours. Squeeze eggplant dry.

Beat egg, grated cheese, salt, and pepper. Dip eggplant into the mixture, and fry out in oil. Brown on both sides. Use 1 pint tomato sauce, a layer of tomatoes, and grated cheese, and a layer of eggplant, etc. Mozzarella cheese can be used.

On top: Sprinkle tomato and grated cheese. Beat egg, pour over top. Bake for 1 hour at 375 degrees uncovered. Check in ½ hour.

Tomato and Eggs

Directions

Cook tomato (about ½ quart) for approximately ½ hour. Flavor with garlic. Make like you would for sauce. Cook for about ½ hour.

When ready, heat oil, add tomato, and cook for about ½ hour, then add eggs like sunny-side up. Cover to simmer for a few minutes, and serve.

Pizza Dough

Ingredients

3 to 3 ½ cups of flour

1 package of yeast (1 tablespoon)

2 teaspoons salt

1 cup warm water

2 tablespoons oil

1+ teaspoon sugar

Directions

Mix ingredients together thoroughly and knead the dough until smooth.

Sweet Dough

Ingredients

1 ½ cups oil

1 ½ cups sugar

1 ½ cups water or milk

6 eggs

5 teaspoons baking powder

Dash of salt

1 teaspoon vanilla

Mix in enough flour to make dough firm, with enough consistency so that it can be rolled.

Directions

Roll on a floured board.

Date Nut Bread

Ingredients

1 cup chopped pitted dates

1 ½ cups boiling water

1 egg

¾ cup of sugar

2 ¼ cups sifted all-purpose flour

2 teaspoons baking soda

¼ teaspoon baking powder

½ teaspoon salt

1 cup chopped nuts (walnuts)

1 tablespoon shortening, melted

1 tablespoon vanilla extract

Directions

Place dates in bowl and pour boiling water over them. Let stand while preparing other ingredients. Beat egg until light and add sugar gradually. Sift together flour, salt, baking powder and baking soda. Stir in walnuts. Add egg and flour mixture alternately to egg mixture. Stir in shortening and vanilla. Pour in a greased loaf pan. Bake at 350 degrees for 1 ¼ hours.

Lasagna

Ingredients

Cut sausage

Cut meatballs

Lasagna sauce

Grated cheese

Layers of lasagna (3)

Directions

Boil water. Add a little oil. Put lasagna strips in one by one to prevent sticking together. Add salt. Boil lasagna rapidly for 15 minutes. Drain like macaroni.

Add a layer of a little meatballs and sausage. Add a layer of mozzarella cheese. Spoon ricotta here and there over the meatballs and sausage. Add a layer of lasagna. Add a layer of meatballs and sausage, mozzarella and ricotta. The top layer is lasagna, sauce, and cheese (mozzarella and grated cheese).

Bake at 350 degrees for 20-25 minutes, with foil on.

Ricotta Dumplings

Directions

Brown garlic in oil. Remove garlic when browned. Add water and parsley. Cover and let boil. Add salt.

Mix in bowl: ricotta, parsley, 1 egg, grated mozzarella, grated parmesan cheese, salt, and bread crumbs. Make little balls.

After the water boils a while, ease balls into water. Let cook about 10 minutes.

Stuffed Cabbage

Directions

Partially cook rice, parboil cabbage just until it can be easily rolled, and drain. Dice salt pork. Use slightly more than ¼ pound of salt pork – fry out in pan with cabbage and fry out onion.

Fix hamburger in a macaroni pan. Blend hamburger and rice, salt and pepper, fresh parsley, onion, 1 egg, salt pork, and diced green pepper (optional). Mix until consistent. Pour off excess grease.

Stuff cabbage and put in pan. Add about ½ quart of tomatoes and water, until the level of the cabbage. Cook on high heat until this boils, then simmer for at least 1 hour to 1 ½ hours.

Spitz-i-olse

Directions

Season meat and oregano, garlic, salt, and pepper. Brown meat and onion on top of stove in olive oil. Add tomato sauce (not a whole can). Let meat simmer. Mushrooms optional. Add water or sauce if it dries out. Add potato when meat is partially cooked.

Braciole

Ingredients

Meat in thin strips

Salt and pepper

Fresh parsley

Grated parmesan cheese

Capers (soak first, for about ½ hour)

Salt pork

Directions

Mix ingredients together and place on flat strips of meat. Roll up and tie with string. Brown. Then put in sauce and cook about 1 hour on simmer. Cover with sauce.

Veal Cacciatore

Ingredients

Veal

Tomato

Green pepper

Onion

Oil

Oregano

Salt

Garlic salt

Pepper

Celery

Parsley

Mushrooms

Directions

Cut veal into small chunks. Brown veal and onions. Cover to brown. Cook with vent open at 325 to 350 degrees. Add celery and seasonings. Cook to simmer and then close vent. Add tomato and mushrooms. Check often, adding water to prevent drying. Stir. In the last 20 minutes, add green peppers and parsley. Cook for 1 ½ hours.

Baked Stuffed Peppers

Ingredients

Green peppers

Hamburger

Garlic salt

Parsley

Bread (soaked and squeezed)

Grated parmesan cheese (1 ½ handfuls)

Crumbled basil leaves

Oregano

Salt

Pepper

2 eggs per pound of hamburger

Onion, chopped

Directions

Cut the peppers in half and stuff them with this mixture. Bake at 375 degrees for 1 hour. Cover with tomato before baking and put oil in bottom of pan. Turn meat-side down when halfway done. Turn back up before finishing. Spoon tomatoes over the top.

Sausage and Peppers

Directions

Cook tomato. Melt lard or use oil if necessary. Brown sausage and remove from pan. Brown peppers and fry out onions. Put sausage, onions, seasonings, and tomato in pan. Cook about ¾ to 1 hour. Then add peppers and cook until done.

Baked Stuffed Lobsters

Ingredients

Bread crumbs

Parsley

Minced clams

Grated cheese

Garlic powder

Salt

Melted butter

Shot of whiskey

Directions

Cut and clean the lobsters. Spoon whiskey and melted butter onto lobster cavity. Mix stuffing ingredients together and stuff lobsters. Put a pat of butter on top and extra bread crumbs. Put water in baking pan. Bake at 300 degrees for 20-25 minutes.

Crab Cakes

Ingredients

½ pound of crab meat

½ teaspoon Old Bay Seasonings

Pinch of salt

1 teaspoon mayonnaise

½ teaspoon Worcestershire Sauce

½ tablespoon chopped parsley

1 teaspoon baking powder

1 egg, beaten

2 slices of bread with crust removed

Directions

Break bread into small pieces and moisten with milk.

Mix ingredients and shape into cakes. Fry until brown.

Baked Scallops

Directions

Dip scallops in beaten egg and parmesan cheese and bread crumbs. Put bread crumbs in a separate dish from cheese and egg. Pour oil into the bottom of a baking dish, and pour in scallops. Put margarine on top. Bake for 45 minutes (approximately) at 400 degrees.

Almond Crescents

Ingredients

1 cup soft shortening

1/3 cup sugar

2/3 cup ground blanched almonds

1 2/3 cups sifted flour

¼ teaspoon salt

Cinnamon

Confectioner's sugar

Directions

Mix thoroughly and sift together. Work in flour and salt. Chill dough. Roll to pencil thickness. Cut in 2 ½ inch lengths. Make crescents on an ungreased baking sheet. Bake until set. When warm, dip in 1 cup confectionary sugar and 1 teaspoon cinnamon, mixed. Bake at 325 degrees for 14 to 16 minutes. Makes about 5 dozen cookies.

Chocolate Raisin Nut Cookies

Ingredients

4 ½ cups flour

2 cups Crisco

2 teaspoons vanilla

2 teaspoons salt

2 teaspoons baking powder

1 ½ cup brown sugar

1 ½ cup white sugar

4 eggs

1 12 oz. package chocolate bits

1 cup nuts

1 cup raisins

Directions

Sift dry ingredients. Cream sugars and Crisco. Add eggs, vanilla, and 1 teaspoon warm water. Add flour mixture. Add chips, nuts, raisins. Mix well. Drop by teaspoon on lightly greased cookie sheet. Bake at 350 degrees for 10 minutes.

Butterballs

Ingredients

1 cup (2 sticks) margarine

1 teaspoon vanilla

1 cup finely chopped walnuts

3 tablespoons confectionary sugar

2 cups flour

Directions

Cream margarine and sugar. Add vanilla. Add flour. Mix well. Fold in nuts. Shape into small round balls. Bake in 350 degree oven on ungreased cookie sheet for 10-12 minutes. While hot, roll in confectionary sugar.

Pumpkin Pie

Ingredients

2 eggs beaten

1 can pumpkin

¾ cup of sugar

1 teaspoon allspice

Pinch of salt

1 ¾ - 2 cups milk (use judgment)

Directions

Mix together in one bowl. Pour into pie shell. Bake at 400 degrees for 40-50 minutes. Knife inserted should come out clean. Serve topped with a dollop of freshly beaten, heavy whipping cream.

Easter Dolls

Ingredients

2 ½ pounds flour

2/3 cup sugar

1 tablespoon salt

Yeast

1 tablespoon shortening dissolved in water

3 eggs, beaten with a fork

2 teaspoons anise seed

2 hardboiled eggs (leave shells on)

Directions

Mix like bread; add beaten egg to dough before baking. Divide the dough into two loaves and roll out in long strips. Twist the dough over one-third of the way from the top, like a ribbon. Add the hardboiled egg in the upper fold of the twist, to make the face of the doll. Add the egg before baking. Bake at 350 degrees. Makes 2 loaves and 2 dolls.

Easter Pies

Ingredients

¾ of a pound of ham

¾ of a pound of prosciuttini

½ pound farmer's cheese

1 small mozzarella

Directions

Cut the ham, prosciuttini, and cheeses into tiny pieces. Mix thoroughly in a bowl.

Dough

Ingredients

6 cups flour

4 eggs

2 good-sized teaspoons baking powder

1 teaspoon salt

1 teaspoon sugar

4 dashes of black pepper

1-2 heaped tablespoons of Crisco

Directions

Blend Crisco into flour, baking powder, salt, sugar, and pepper. Make like cornmeal, with no big lumps in the dough. Break 4 eggs into the mixture. Mix eggs in well. Add salt and water gradually, mixing until dough is pliable. Approximately 1 ½ to 2 cups. Put on board and work the dough. Leave dough covered in bowl.

When ready to use: Grease pans lightly, with shortening. Make like a turnover. Take a fork and punch holes in the top of the loaf. Color the top of the bread with a beaten egg yolk, brushing it on with a pastry brush and making it golden. Bake at 375 for 1 to 1 ¼ hours.

Coda: When Irish Eyes Are Smiling

Just as this book about my Italian-American family begins with a story about my Irish-American mother and great-aunt Nanna, I will conclude with my mother's family recipe for Traditional Irish Soda Bread. The Christmas before she passed away, Mom wrote the recipe out for me by hand, and she included it with a loaf of the bread. Irish Soda Bread was something our mother made for years, and which she especially loved to make on Saint Patrick's Day. Thank you, Mom.

Traditional Irish Soda Bread

Ingredients

3 cups flour

1 teaspoon baking soda

2 tablespoons baking powder

1 teaspoon salt

1 cup raisins

3 tablespoons margarine

1 egg

1 cup of milk

1 shot of rye whiskey

3 tablespoons granulated sugar

Directions

Heat oven to 400 degrees. Blend all ingredients well. Put in a greased loaf pan. Bake 50-60 minutes. Test with a toothpick. If it comes out clean, the bread is baked.

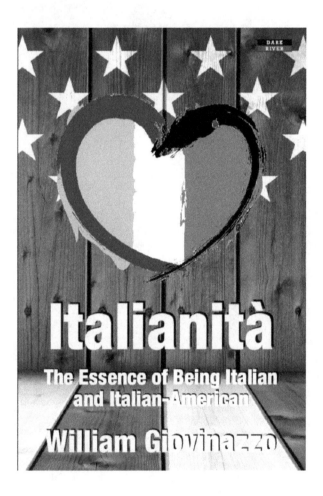

Italianità

The Essence of Being Italian and Italian-American

William Giovinazzo

Italianità: The Essence of Being Italian and Italian-American

Whether we hail from Napoli or New York, Bari or Boston, Poughkeepsie or Palermo, there is a special quality that binds us – *Italiani nel Mondo* – together.

And that agent is *Italianità,* the essence of being Italian.

We are all Italian, but trying to define exactly what that means – what makes us all part of one global family – well, that can be a little tougher.

In this book, William Giovinazzo explores the culture and history of Italians and Italian-Americans, from the time when the Greeks first colonized Italy, to the influx of Italian immigrants in the 19th and 20th centuries, to John Travolta strutting his stuff in a New York disco.

In an insightful and entertaining journey, which also takes in food, religion, relationships, and – of course – the Mafia, we explore how the two groups are the same and how they differ. Ultimately, we discover how *Italianità* is a complex and multifaceted entity; it's what makes Italian and Italian-American societies the wonderful, life-affirming, vibrant cultures that they are.